Madrid

Berlitz Publishing Company, Inc.
Princeton   Mexico City   Dublin   Eschborn   Singapore

Berlitz Trademark Reg. U.S. Patent Office and other countries
Marca Registrada

Text:	Neil Schlecht
Editor:	Media Content Marketing, Inc.
Photography:	Neil Schlecht except pages 9, 10, 14, 37, 54, 61, 63, 64, 72, 77, 81, 82, 88 by Dany Gignoux
Cover Photo:	Neil Schlecht
Photo Editor:	Naomi Zinn
Layout:	Media Content Marketing, Inc.
Cartography:	Ortelius Design

Although the publisher tries to insure the accuracy of all the information in this book, changes are inevitable and errors may result. The publisher cannot be responsible for any resulting loss, inconvenience, or injury. If you find an error in this guide, please let the editors know by writing to Berlitz Publishing Company, 400 Alexander Park, Princeton, NJ 08540-6306.

ISBN 2-8315-7700-4

Printed in Italy
010/010 REV

CONTENTS

- A  in the text denotes a highly recommended sight

Madrid

MADRID AND ITS PEOPLE, THE *MADRILEÑOS*

For a half millennium or more, Madrid idled as a provincial backwater, rarely noticed on the arid central plains of Castile, until Felipe II plucked it from his royal cap in 1561 and proclaimed it the capital of Spain. Man-made Madrid, which quickly assumed the reigns of Spain's Golden Age, hasn't stopped growing and asserting itself since. Though one of Europe's youngest capitals, it's had plenty of time to catch up to Spain's more historic cities, including Seville, Toledo and Granada, and today it is their political, administrative and economic superior. Only Barcelona rivals it in economic importance.

Felipe II's royal decree was based entirely on geography: the idea being that Madrid, smack in the center of Iberia, would promote centralized authority over regional power bases in a newly unified Spain. Today Madrid is that cohesive center and more. It is a city to which people migrate from all over Spain in search of new opportunities; a place where few people can claim any deep roots.

Madrid is a bustling, sprawling, mostly modern metropolis. This capital city of four million is constantly rattled by noise and stifled by dense traffic. As Spain has solidified its place in the European Union, Madrid has become larger, more important, and yes, somewhat less characteristically Iberian. Once, its immigrants were from the surrounding regions of Spain; today, its newcomers are from across Europe and beyond, bringing with them new languages and customs.

Among other parts of Spain, Andalucía is more folkloric, Catalonia and the Basque country more proudly independent. Barcelona and Granada possess greater architecture, and many Spanish cities have finer natural attributes. But Madrileños don't begrudge those places anything. Madrid may be a planned bureaucrat's town (like Brasilia or Washington), but it's far richer in color and tone. Madrid is the next rung down from heaven, so the boastful local saying goes, and the city's residents claim their superiority in other terms.

Madrid reigns in cultural life and *vida nocturna* — nightlife. Few cities have so perfected the art of socializing — eating and drinking — in public. A collective and gregarious lot who seem to carry on much of their lives in the streets, Madrileños are stars when night falls, hopping in and out of *tabernas* and *tascas* (cave-like taverns and bars), for repeated rituals of *tapas* (bar finger-foods), jugs of Spanish wine, and hyper-animated conversation. The night goes late — very late — in Madrid, and there's not a day of the week that the streets aren't flooded by hordes of after-hours diners and bar-hoppers. A lack of sleep can always be remedied later, a Madrileño might tell you, as he tops off a late night with early-morning *chocolate con curros* (a fried-dough and chocolate snack ideal for absorbing alcohol) on the way home for a shower and then continues on to work.

The night's rowdy revelers get most of the attention — surely Madrid must pack in more bars, discos and live-music venues per capita than any other sizeable European city. Yet the city also makes plenty of room for more elevated pursuits including Spain's most sophisticated cultural life: opera, theater, *zarzuela* (an indigenous form of light comic opera), and dance. These entertainments flourish, as does flamenco, a popular art form with spiritual callings, for both the purist and the tourist.

Madrid's cultural output reaches its apogee, though, in its superb concentration of art museums. On one grand boulevard, the Paseo del Prado, are three of Europe's finest museums: the world-class Prado museum, the Thyssen-Bornemisza collection, and the Centro de Arte Reina Sofía (Queen Sofía Art Center), whose claim to fame is the 20th century's most famous painting, Pablo Picasso's *Guernica*. Madrid's collection of

Spanish Old Masters — Velázquez, El Greco, Goya, Zurbarán, and more — is unrivalled in the world.

Though a city of immigrants, the city clings to *castizo* (working-class Madrileño) traditions. Madrid is the focus of that fiercest of Spanish customs, the bullfight, and local *ferias* and *fiestas* like San Isidro, a celebration of the city's patron saint, are prepared and attended with the same zeal that they are in small Spanish towns. In fact, in the relatively small area that most visitors are likely to cover, Madrid doesn't really feel like an overgrown, Europeanized capital. With its

Families can watch an endless succession of rowboats in Retiro Park.

friendly taverns, street booksellers, and mom-and-pop shops, it frequently seems like a small — albeit densely populated-Spanish town, and it is easily covered on foot.

The heart of the city is Viejo Madrid, Old Madrid, a largely 16th-century city built upon the layout of narrow, winding streets of an old Moorish settlement. "Madrid de los Asturias" is named for the Hapsburgs instrumental in the city's rapid growth during the 1600s. Old Madrid's centerpiece is its splendid, porticoed and sun-glazed Plaza Mayor. Little remains of medieval Madrid, but there are glimpses of the oldest parts of the city in the Arab walls and several attractive small plazas, as well as many other discoveries to be made in this area that extends from the River Manzanares and Palacio Real (Royal Palace, actually the legacy of the later Bourbon rulers) to the lively, congested Puerta del Sol, still the nerve center of Madrid.

The Bourbon monarchs of the 18th century fostered Madrid's expansion east. They built monumental Madrid, a city of grand avenues and boulevards, fountains, gateways, and parks. Bourbon Madrid is best symbolized by the handsome Paseo del Prado and Parque del Buen Retiro, once the royal family's private park and hunting grounds.

Modern Madrid grew unrelentingly in all directions beginning in the 19th century. Its most attractive nucleus is the neighborhood of Salamanca, an elite *barrio* of tony apartment buildings and sophisticated designer shops. La Castellana and Paseo de Recoletos are continuations north of the Prado boulevard of the Bourbons. Both are lined with sidewalk cafes and strollers on sunny days and summer nights. Madrid spilled outward from

Real life, or postcard? The Madrid skyline portrays both a major European capital and a city of dreams.

there, and, especially in the last two decades, has pushed farther and farther out, leaving little distinction between city and suburb.

Madrid's diverse architecture, while not the equal of a Paris or London, traces the city's stages of expansion and prevailing styles of the different eras. Moving outward from the center, one passes from stately, ornamental 16th-century apartment buildings with shuttered windows, wrought-iron balconies, and brick facades to the Baroque palaces of the Bourbons, and later Neo-classical buildings meant to convey authority. The elegant (and today traffic-choked) Gran Vía, Madrid's central shopping artery, is a turn-of-the century showcase of Art Nouveau and Art Deco styles.

Madrid is at the forefront of a new, dynamic Spain. After tossing off the shackles of Franco's long dictatorship that isolated Spain from the rest of Europe, Madrid erupted from the closet, embracing a frenetic arts and nightlife scene called *la movida* in the early 1980s. Homosexuality, drugs, all-night partying, and living life on the edge (the credo of films by Pedro Almodóvar, the boy wonder of la movida), were the shocking symbols of the new Spain. Once unshakingly traditional, conservative, and Catholic, a country where official awards used to be given for fecundity, Spain today has the fewest children in Europe. Its population is actually dwindling, as women assert themselves in careers and couples contemplate the economic challenges of raising a family in a congested and competitive city like Madrid.

Still, the Spain of yesteryear flourishes in many corners of the city. At the hour of the *paseo* (stroll)*,* when offices empty, *Madrileños* spill onto promenades and swamp outdoor cafés, plunging into conversation. Conservatively dressed businessmen escort impeccably coiffed women, while retired gentlemen in cardigans, jackets and ties play chess or *petanca* (a game resembling marbles, but played with heavy shot-puts) in the park. Locals of all ages, from senior citizens to high-school kids donning Metallica T-shirts, crowd into 18th-century taverns to sip sherry or *vino tinto* drawn from old wooden barrels, and to munch on morsels of *tortilla española*.

Madrid's easy embrace of extremes — it is both the capital of a technology-dependent country that exploded since becoming part of the European Union just 15 years ago and at heart a small town that revels in its castizo traditions — is part of life here. Even nature imposes extremes. At an altitude of more than 640 meters (2,100 feet), this city on the Castilian plateau, Europe's highest capital, is scorching in summer, when wilting residents flee for the coast or cooler northern climes, and freezing in winter, when many Madrileños bolt for the Sierra Nevada, just a couple hours south, to ski.

Escaping after a few days in the capital is the plan of most visitors as well; for most, a trip to Madrid is as much about what the plains of Castile just beyond the city contain as what the capital itself offers. Madrid is the perfect base for explorations into the heart and soul of Spain, with a wealth of fascinating day trips and a trio of UNESCO-honored cities just an hour or so from the city. Toledo, Spain's former capital set on a crag above a river moat, is a living museum of El Greco and the legacy of a great capital city of Christians, Jews, and Muslims. Segovia is a picture postcard of central Spain, a royal stronghold with a fairy-tale castle and astounding 2,000-year-old Roman aqueduct. The walled city of Ávila is the birthplace of the mystic St. Theresa, who still commands intense devotion among her followers.

Closer to Madrid are other sights that reveal pivotal periods of Spanish history. El Escorial is a dramatic monastery, mausoleum, and palace built by Felipe II, and one of the most-visited places in Spain; and nearby is El Valle de los Caídos (Valley of the Fallen), Franco's memorial to his reign and soldiers killed in the Civil War of 1936–1939.

A BRIEF HISTORY

Though prehistoric remains from the Paleolithic, Neolithic, and Bronze Ages have been unearthed in the Manzanares Valley, prior to Madrid's sudden elevation to capital city in 1561 its history was rather undistinguished.

Over a period of many centuries crucial in Spanish history, Madrid's significance was negligible. The Romans built their most advanced outpost on the Iberian peninsula, but left nothing of consequence in Madrid. Armies of North African nomads, intent on disseminating Islam, invaded the peninsula in A.D. 711. Within 10 years, they had overrun most of Spain. If Madrid played any role in these pivotal events, no record of it remains.

The first solid references to this obscure settlement on the Castilian plateau, guarded by the looming Guadarrama mountain range, appear in the 9th century. The Arabic name for "place of many springs," variously recorded as Magerit, Mayrit or Magrit, eventually evolved into Madrid. The hamlet entered historical chronicles for its military significance; it was located near the main line of resistance to the Christian reconquest. Over centuries of struggle, the defending Moorish army built a full-scale fort, or *Alcázar,* on the heights of Madrid commanding the Manzanares valley.

After several unsuccessful skirmishes, the Christian forces of Alfonso VI captured Madrid in 1083. The Alcázar became a fort of the crown of Castile. During a counter-offensive in 1109, the town was overrun by the Moors, but the Christianized fortress held. The Moors were expelled from the town, but they remained in control of southern Spain for almost four centuries.

Meanwhile, Madrid enjoyed brief prominence in 1308 when king Ferdinand IV and his *Cortes*, an early version of

*Autos pass over the bridge at Puente Segovia —
modernity coupled with Madrid's medieval past.*

parliament, held a formal meeting in the fledgling town. From then on, the kings of Spain began to visit Madrid, where the air was invigorating and the hunting excellent.

Ferdinand and Isabella, the Catholic monarchs that united all the provinces of Spain, first visited Madrid in 1477. They appreciated the town's loyalty to the crown, but the idea never occurred to anyone, let alone the two monarchs, that Madrid might one day become the capital. Historically important Toledo seemed secure in the role.

Spain's Golden Age

Under Ferdinand and Isabella, Spain underwent a dramatic transformation. In 1492 the royal pair presided over the final conquest over the Moors and discovery of the New World, including the great wealth that feat brought to Spain. Spain flourished during a Golden Age, a century of Spanish economic and political supremacy in international affairs, accompanied by marvels of art and literature.

Ferdinand and Isabella were consummate Spaniards, committed to the expansion of the crown. By contrast, their grandson, who assumed the throne in 1516, was born in Flanders in 1500, and Charles I could barely express himself in Spanish. The first of the Habsburgs, he packed his retinue with Burgundian and Flemish nobles.

Soon after his arrival in Spain, the young man inherited the title of Holy Roman Emperor, as Charles V. The responsibilities of the crown kept him busy away from the royal residences of Toledo, Segovia, Valladolid, and Madrid. While the monarch was away on one of his many business trips, his increasingly dissatisfied subjects protested violently. A revolt of the *comuneros,* or townsmen, broke out in a number of Spanish cities, including Madrid. The rebels occupied the alcázar, which had by then been converted to a royal palace. The insurrection was quashed and its leaders executed, but the king got the message. He tried thereafter to pay more attention to his Spanish constituency.

Man of Action, Man of Letters

Miguel de Cervantes Saavedra fought at the Battle of Lepanto (1571) and was wounded, captured, and imprisoned. He escaped, was enslaved and finally ransomed. Returning to Spain, he worked as an army quartermaster but spent several spells in jail on financial charges. Then, at the age of 58, he wrote his masterwork and the world's bestselling novel, *Don Quixote.* In his modest house in Madrid's calle del León, Cervantes died on April 23, 1616.

Madrid's Rise to Capital

In 1556, Charles abdicated in favor of his son, Felipe II, good news for Spain and even better for Madrid. Felipe moved the royal court from Toledo to Madrid in 1561, converting an unimpressive town of less than 15,000 people into the capital of the world's greatest empire. Madrid soared onward and upward, increasing nearly eightfold in population; Spain's fortunes as a whole were more volatile. Felipe II took credit for a rousing naval victory at Lepanto, teaming with Venetians against the Turks, but less than two decades later Spain was subjected to the humiliating defeat of its "invincible" armada, at the hands of Sir Francis Drake and a small English navy. Felipe II's greatest lasting legacy is El Escorial, a grandiose palace and monastery in the foothills of the Sierra de Guadarrama, northwest of Madrid.

Felipe's son, Felipe III, was unfaithful to Spain's new capital. For several years he held court in Valladolid, though eventually he returned to Madrid. It was he who ordered the construction of the Plaza Mayor, the magnificent main square that still dignifies the center of the Viejo Madrid. Other tasteful, 17th-century buildings constructed nearby, such as the foreign ministry and town hall, reveal that the capital was at last being taken seriously.

The Habsburgs bowed out in 1700 with the death of Charles II. The subsequent war over Spanish succession resulted in the enthronement of the Bourbon candidate, Felipe V. When Madrid's alcázar burned down in 1734, with the loss of many art treasures, Felipe seized the opportunity to build a new, incredibly lavish royal palace. Madrid's Palacio Real is still used on occasion by King Juan Carlos I for official ceremonies.

Madrid owes much to the civic-mindedness of Charles III, who ruled from 1759 to 1788. He paved and lighted the streets, installed public fountains, built the Prado museum, and laid out vast promenades and gardens.

Francisco de Goya painted a court portrait of the next king, Charles IV, in which he looked strangely like George Washington. But Charles was considerably less successful politically than his transatlantic contemporary. His 20-year reign, weak at best, ended in all-round disaster: abdication, arrest, and war.

Spain again became a battleground in the early 1800s, with British forces taking on Napoleon's troops in the Peninsular War. Napoleon invaded Spain in March 1808 and invested his older, taller, and more agreeable brother, Joseph, as King José I. On May 2, 1808, Madrid rose up against the interloper. The Peninsular War (called the War of Independence by Spaniards) went on murderously but inconclusively for six years. Finally, with the help of the British under the duke of Wellington, the Spanish expelled the occupying forces. In truth, Joseph Bonaparte meant well — he built so many plazas that *Madrileños* nicknamed him *El Rey Plazuelas* — but the people loathed a government imposed from abroad. José I spent 17 years of exile in, of all unlikely places, New Jersey.

Spanish royalty presides over the Plaza de Oriente, built in the 19th century.

Decline and Decadence

The son of Charles IV, Fernando VII, was seated on his rightful throne in the Royal Palace of Madrid in 1814. But the war and the repercussions of the French Revolution had helped to create in Spain the nucleus of a liberal national party. Power struggles at home and rebellion by colonies abroad ensued.

The spirit of liberalism prevalent in Europe was tardy in reaching Spain. After many reverses, a democratic constitution was finally proclaimed and constitutional monarchy was instituted in 1874. By the time of the Spanish–American War of 1898, the Spanish empire of the Golden Age had been whittled to insignificance. King Alfonso XIII, who linked the 19th and 20th centuries, inaugurated the Madrid Metro (underground railway) and University City. But he was undone by the chronic unrest of his subjects. Neither constitutional government nor dictatorship proved workable, and in 1931 the king went into exile following anti-royalist results in municipal elections.

The Civil War

In 1931, general elections brought the Republicans to power, and King Alfonso XIII escaped in exile. In the new Republic, bitter ideological conflicts divided parties and factions, and the church was also involved. For the next several years the pendulum of power in Spain swung back and forth between Left and Right.

Finally, in 1936, a large section of the army under General Francisco Franco rose in revolt against the government. On Franco's side were monarchists, conservatives, the Catholic Church, and the right-wing Falangists. United against him was a collection of republicans, liberals, socialists, commu-

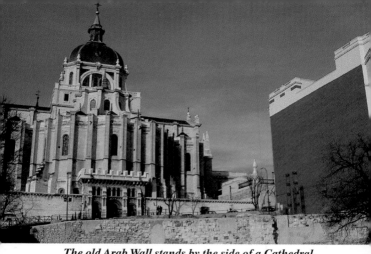

The old Arab Wall stands by the side of a Cathedral, exhibiting Madrid's two disparate religious traditions.

nists, and anarchists. The civil war developed into one of the great causes of the 20th century, with support for both sides pouring in from outside of Spain. Often unaware of the particular Spanish origins of the struggle, many Europeans saw the civil war as a crucial conflict between democracy and dictatorship, or from the other side, as a conflict between law and order and the forces of social revolution and chaos.

The war was brutal and bloody, and both sides committed atrocities. The Civil War ended with some 700,000 combatants dead on both sides; another 30,000 were executed or assassinated, including many priests and nuns, and perhaps 15,000 civilians were killed in air raids. Madrid remained in Republican hands for most of the war, but the government was evacuated in the early stages of a nationalist siege that lasted until March 1939.

Even when the war ended, the hardship continued. Despite Hitler's efforts at persuasion, Spain's new *caudillo* (strongman), Generalísimo Franco, managed to keep Spain out of World War II. Spain was admitted to the United Nations in 1955, opening the gates to an overwhelming tourist invasion, which would have profound effects on both the economy and national mentality.

When Franco died in 1975, Spain rapidly emerged from its isolation. The coronation of his designated successor, Juan Carlos, the grandson of Alfonso XIII, brought the restoration of parliamentary democracy and a relaxation of customs and laws. The king's commitment to democracy brought Spain into line with the rest of Western Europe and assured it of membership in the European Union, which was granted in 1986. Madrid flourished in the early 1980s, as characterized by *la movida,* a hip cultural explosion that rejected the repression of the Franco era through acts of hedonism and creative films, music and theater.

Charismatic Felipe González, a Socialist, was Prime Minister of Spain from 1982 to 1986. Spain became a member of the European Economic Community (now called European Union, or EU) in 1986, hastening the country's modernization. In a single year, 1992, Spain dominated the world stage: Barcelona hosted the Summer Olympic Games, Seville the World Expo, and Madrid held the role of European Cultural Capital.

Though González was credited by many as the architect of the new Spain, he finally succumbed to incessant charges of corruption and incompetence in the highest levels of his government. In 1996, the surging Partido Popular, led by a decidely uncharismatic former accountant, José María Aznar, was elected, forming the first conservative government in Spain since the return of democracy.

Historical Landmarks

900–400 B.C. Celtic tribes settle and mix with indigenous Iberians.

206 B.C. Romans defeat Carthaginians.

711 A.D. Moorish invasion of Spain.

852 Moors found settlement of mayerit.

932 Madrid occupied by Christian king, Ramiro II.

996 Madrid conquered by Castile.

1109 Moors unsuccessfully storm Madrid. Madrid wins status of town.

1309 Royal Parliament (Cortes) held in Madrid.

1469 Marriage of Ferdinand and Isabella unites Aragón and Catalonia with Castile to create a unified Spain.

1492 Moors defeated in Granada; Muslims and Jews expelled.

1516 Charles I (Charles V, Holy Roman Emperor) takes throne.

1561 Felipe II establishes capital in Madrid, replacing Toledo.

1600 Felipe III briefly moves capital to Valladolid.

1606 Madrid renamed capital of Spain.

1701–1713 War of Spanish Succession.

1808–1814 Peninsular War between England and Napoleonic France; Joseph Bonaparte becomes king.

1835 Sequestration of church properties.

1875 Restoration of Bourbon monarchy.

1931 Republican party comes to power.

1936–1939 Spanish Civil War ends in Franco dictatorship. Spain isolated from rest of Europe.

1975 Franco dies, Juan Carlos becomes king.

1980s Regions receive limited autonomous rule.

1986 Spain joins European Community (now European Union).

1992 Summer Olympics in Barcelona; World Expo in Seville; Madrid serves as European Cultural Capital.

1997 Conservative Partido Popular's José María Aznar elected.

2000 José María Aznar and conservative Partido Popular (Popular Party) reelected for second four-year term.

WHERE TO GO

In this sprawling city, the parts of Madrid of greatest interest to foreign visitors are remarkably compact. Viejo Madrid, the city of the Hapsburgs, covers a small area that extends east from the pitiful Río Manzanares and magnificent Palacio Real to Puerta del Sol. Almost all of it can be covered in a day or two, including a lengthy visit to the Royal Palace. The Madrid of the Bourbon dynasty, home to Spain's great art museums, is the next area worthy of exploring (for art lovers, though, it may very well be the first). Spain's Golden Triangle of Art is concentrated on the elegant but busy Paseo del Prado, between Puerta del Sol and Retiro Park. Those with more time in Madrid, either before or after side trips to the great towns of Castile, might explore the barrio of Salamanca, take in a bull-fight, or visit one or more of the smaller, more personal muse-ums, only a ride from the Puerta del Sol.

VIEJO MADRID (OLD MADRID)

Viejo Madrid, the area spreading outward from the Plaza Mayor, is the sentimental and geographical heart of the city. After Madrid became the seat of the royal court, this area grew rapidly in the 16th and 17th centuries. Its cobblestoned streets are full of atmospheric *tascas* (tapas bars) and restau-rants, and they contain several of the city's most important sights, including the Royal Palace, Plaza Mayor, Puerta del Sol, and Monasterio de las Decalzas Reales, Madrid's most important convent.

Few buildings and monuments from medieval Madrid ex-ist, but the mood still does. It's palpable in the narrow streets that meander south from the calle Mayor (Main Street) and quiet plazas in and around La Latina. Dimly lit shops continue to dispense what they always have: books, cheese, religious

*A statue of Felipe III presides over the Plaza Mayor —
an ideal starting point for a tour of old Madrid.*

statues, and military medals. Outside a tavern you may see a waiter pin up a hand-written menu, or a blind lottery-ticket seller tapping his white cane to attract attention, reciting the day's lucky numbers.

The porticoed **Plaza Mayor** (main square), an architectural symphony in bold but balanced tones, is one of Spain's most recognizable sights. Broad arcades surround a cobbled rectangle 200 meters long and 100 meters wide (656 ft x 328 ft). It was built in the beginning of the 17th century, based on the graceful style of Juan de Herrera (Felipe II's architect, responsible for El Escorial): symmetry, slate roofs, and slender towers. The Plaza Mayor may be entered by any of nine archways, but mercifully not by motorized vehicles. The square was once the scene of pageants, lively marketplaces, theater festivals, bullfights, religious processions, and even trials and executions during the Spanish Inquisition — residents with access to any of the 400 balconies overlooking the square used to sell tickets for such events. A statue of Felipe III, who ordered the plaza to be built, occupies the place of honor, and the Casa de la Panadería (bakery) is decorated with colorful frescoes above the arcades. Even if you've only just begun your tour of Madrid, the Plaza is a great spot for taking in the proportions of Madrid's most elegant architectural ensemble from a seat at one of the outdoor cafés.

> Street addresses in Madrid place the street number after the street name and the floor and apartment number after that. For example: calle Mayor, 15 2-4, means building number 15, second floor, apartment or office number 4. Street, *calle*, is abbreviated "*c/*"; promenade or boulevard, *Paseo (Po); avenue, Avenida (Av.).*

Leading out of each of the arched doorways of the Plaza is a maze of small, winding streets — the most famous of which is **Cava San Miguel** — lined with shops, taverns, and *mesones* (cave-like bars). But if you stick to calle Mayor heading west, you'll first come to **Mercado de San Miguel**, a food and produce market established in 1915.

Farther along c/ Mayor is Madrid's oldest square, **Plaza de la Villa** (City Hall Square). This fascinating juxtaposition of stately 16th- and 17th-century buildings was once the Moors' central market square. The 15th-century Gothic **Casa y Torre de los Lujanes** (House and Tower of the Lujanes) has an imposing stone portal and *mudéjar* tower. **Casa de Cisneros,** on the south side of the square, was built in the mid-16th century by a nephew of the intrepid inquisitor and warrior, Cardinal Cisneros, and is a fine example of the ornate and delicate style of Spanish early Renaissance architecture known as Plateresque. The **Ayuntamiento** (City Hall) building, connected by passageway, represents the Hapsburg era, with the towers and slate spires characteristic of the 17th-century official buildings common in this district of Madrid.

At the end of c/ Mayor, just past c/ Bailén, is **Parque Emir Mohammed I,** where you can still see fragments of the old Moorish wall that encircled the Mayerit settlement.

South of Plaza de la Villa and calle Segovia is the neighborhood called **La Latina** and the old Moorish district, La Morería, where the intense traffic and bustle of Madrid suddenly subsides. The quiet and pretty square, **Plaza de la Paja** (Straw Square), was the commercial focus of the city in the days before the Plaza Mayor. On the south side of the plaza, with its entrance around the other side, is **Iglesia de San Andrés** (Church of St. Anthony's), now splendidly restored after a decade of work. Two adjoining chapels, Capilla del Obispo (Bishop's chapel) and Capilla de San Isidro, the first Gothic and the second Baroque, are also worth a look.

A formidable Madrid church of the mid-18th century is southwest of here, the **Basílica de San Francisco El Grande** (Basilica of St. Francis of Assisi). The curved

Casa y Torre de los Lujanes, at the center of Plaza de la Villa.

façade, an original version of a Neo-classical design, somewhat curtails the effect of the church's most superlative feature, its extraordinary dome. Indeed, its inner diameter of more than 31 m (100 ft) exceeds the size of the cupolas of St. Paul's in London and Les Invalides in Paris). Oversized statues of the apostles in white marble are stationed around the rotunda, and seven richly ornamented chapels fan out from the center. The church's painting collection includes an early Goya.

Just east of Plaza San Andrés is a jumble of some of Madrid's most animated streets, **Cava Baja, Cava Alta, Almendro,** and **calle del Nuncio,** the heart of La Latina. Just about every address in this district houses an appealing old tavern or tasca. The barrio is one of Madrid's classic working-class areas. The popular **El Rastro fleamarket** is held every Sunday

The gates of the majestic and voluminous Palacio Real beckon to visitors to come inside.

along the warren of streets near calle de Toledo, a lively thoroughfare that leads back up to the Plaza Mayor. Nearby is the **Catedral de San Isidro**, built in the early 1600s and long the provisional cathedral of Madrid. There are more than 200 churches in Madrid, though in this country replete with spectacular cathedrals and churches, few are essen-

> *Mudéjar* **architecture refers to a style made popular after the Christian reconquest of Spain. Christians employed Moorish (Muslim) craftsmen to design and construct buildings, which retained many Moorish aspects.**

tial sights. Madrid is simply too young a city to have a great medieval cathedral. San Isidro has a massive dome, a single nave and, among many relics, the revered remains of the city's patron saint, San Isidro Labrador.

Palacio Real (Royal Palace)

The Royal Palace, just west of the Plaza de Oriente, is geographically part of Old Madrid, even if was not built until the 18th century. The palace was ordered by the Bourbon king Felipe V and completed by Carlos III. Set among formal gardens on a bluff overlooking the Manzanares valley, on the site of the old Moorish fortress (which burned down in 1734), the immense and imperious residence is loaded with art and history.

Guided and self-guided tours of the palace take in only a fraction of the 2,000 rooms (more than any other palace in Europe), though many of the highlights are visited. The first feature visitors see is the immense **Plaza de la Armería**, which overlooks the valley west of Madrid. The entrance to the palace is via the main staircase — bright, airy, and ceremonious beneath an arched ceiling. Each step is a single slab of marble. The **Salón de los Halberdiers** contains remarkably preserved ancient Flemish and Spanish tapestries. The **Salón del Trono** (Throne Room) occupies the very center of the south façade of the palace. Red velvet and mirrors in matching gilt frames cover the walls. The ceiling was painted by Tiepolo in 1764. Gilded bronze lions defend the throne. The conversation antechamber, contributed by Carlos III, has four handsome Goya portraits.

The apartments of Carlos III consist of one lavish room after another. The outstanding **Salón de Gasparini** is named after the artist (Matias Gasparini of Naples) that mobilized stone-cutters, sculptors, glass-blowers, clock-makers, silversmiths, cabinet-makers, and embroiderers to produce this stunning example of rococo. Floor, walls, and ceiling swirl with special effects. The **Sala de Porcelana** (Porcelain Room) is an overwhelming display of porcelain: more than 1,000 pieces from the Buen Retiro factory of the 18th century.

> As a working palace, the Palacio Real is occasionally closed to the public for official state functions. Ask at the tourist office for the schedule.

The regal, extravagant **Comedor de Gala** (Ceremonial Dining Room), built for the wedding of Alfonso XII and his second wife, María Cristina in 1879, seats 145 guests. Notice the 15 chandeliers, 10 candelabra, and 18th-century Chinese porcelain jars along walls hung with Brussels tapestries.

After visiting the main building, see the **Botica Real** (Royal Pharmacy). Built in 1594, the pharmacy's cupboards line two rooms with matching glass and porcelain apothecary jars specially ordered by Carlos IV. Also part of this annex is the **Armería Real** (Royal Armory). Swashbuckling swordsmen and jousting horsemen are commemorated here in a display of authentic battle flags, trophies, shields, and weapons. The armory is officially called the finest collection of its type in the world. The **Biblioteca Real** (Royal Library) is not generally open to the public, but special access is allowed for approved researchers.

Madrid's lovely opera house — the Teatro Real — figures prominently in the Plaza de Oriente.

Just east of the Royal Palace is the stately **Plaza de Oriente,** lined with statues of Spanish kings and queens, and the **Teatro Real,** Madrid's long-suffering opera house. Built in the mid-19th century, it has been beset by all kinds of funding and structural problems. It finally reopened, after a decade-long and extravagantly budgeted restoration, in 1999.

A couple of blocks north is the **Convento de la Encarnación** (Convent of the Incarnation), on the plaza of the same name. Founded in 1611 by Margarita de Austria, this convent has accumulated an interesting art collection, including a gruesome wooden sculpture of Christ after his crucifixion — bloody, blue-lipped, with his eyes rolling back into his head. The most fascinating feature, though, is the reliquary, lined with religious relics, some also rather macabre. In the 18th-century Baroque church, you may hear the nuns praying or singing, but you'll never see them; they are cloistered on the other side of the grillwork.

Nearby (and possible to visit on a joint ticket with the Convento de la Incarnación) is the **Monasterio de Las Descalzas Reales** (Monastery of the Barefoot Royal Ladies). Though one of Madrid's top sights, many visitors still miss it. The former medieval palace clings to a 16th-century tranquillity. Founded by princess Juana de Austria, the daughter of Holy Roman Emperor Carlos V, in 1566, the palace was transformed into a convent by the architect responsible for El Escorial. Subsidized by generous patrons, the convent accepted only nuns of the highest nobility until the beginning of the 18th century. The wealthy sisters brought with them spectacular works of art and statues of baby Jesus. Cloistered Franciscan nuns — a maximum of 33 (the age of Jesus when he died) but today far fewer — remain on the premises but stay out of sight

Be sure not to miss the Monasterio de Las Descalzas Realas, an authentic remnant of the 16th century.

during visiting hours. Until 30 years ago, the convent was completely cloistered — no visits allowed.

Visitors' first views of the convent's splendor begin with the theatrical granite stairway, splashed with splendid 17th-century frescoes from floor to ceiling. Above the stairway leading upstairs is a depiction of Felipe IV and his family. On the second floor are heavy timbered ceilings and walls covered with works of art, mostly of religious or royal significance. In one hall, there are a dozen splendid 17th-century tapestries based on original Rubens drawings. The museum contains outstanding paintings by Titian, Brueghel the Elder, and Zurbarán. The shrine of the convent church is particularly well endowed in religious relics and jewels.

Near the Puerta del Sol

Puerta del Sol (Gateway to the Sun) is Madrid's busiest plaza and for centuries has been the commercial hub of the city. Today it marks the transition between Hapsburg Madrid and the city expansion of the Bourbon kings. The original gate that once existed here — part of the ancient town wall — was torn down in 1570. Ten streets converge on the plaza, and all the radial highways of Spain are measured from Puerta del Sol, designated "Kilometer Zero" (on the sidewalk on the south side of the square is a symbol of this distinction).

The no-nonsense, Neo-classical building on the south side of the square (Casa de Correos) houses the main offices of the regional government. Thousands of *Madrileños* gather here for a ritual every New Year's Eve. They try to swallow a dozen grapes while the clock atop the building strikes 12, after which pandemonium breaks out.

Facing all the bustle of a remodeled Puerta del Sol is a statue based on Madrid's coat of arms, which depicts a bear leaning against a *madroño* tree (an arbutus, or strawberry tree). The bear is a symbol of Madrid, while the Tío Pepe sign, an advertisement for one of Spain's most famous brands of sherry, has become the unofficial symbol of the Puerta del Sol.

Just north of the Puerta del Sol and next door to the Ministry of Finance, is the **Real Academia de Bellas Artes de San Fernando —** call it the Museum of the Royal Academy. It possesses a celebrated collection of Goya's paintings, including *Burial of the Sardine,* and a superb self-portrait of the artist in his old age. Velázquez, Murillo, and Rubens are also represented among the hundreds of works on display. The Royal Academy also has a magnificent collection of paintings by Zurbarán, rivaling that of the Prado Museum. Representative of the artist's austere, devotional style is *Vision of the Blessed Alonso Rodríguez.*

Southeast of Puerta del Sol is **Plaza Santa Ana** and the **Huertas** district, both of which are chock full of restaurants, tascas and tapas bars, theaters, and live music and flamenco clubs. The area really springs to life at night.

BOURBON MADRID

West of Puerta del Sol is the city's 18th-century expansion engineered by the Bourbon monarchs. Calle de Alcalá merges with Gran Vía and leads to the Plaza de la Cibeles and the Paseo del Prado,with its trio of art museums. The area's spacious boulevards, grand plazas, and fountains are interspersed with densely populated 18th-century apartment buildings. After hitting the art world's Big Three, visitors can repair to Retiro Park, where kings once found respite from the demands of hectic city life.

Except for the traffic spitting out noise and air pollution, the ample **Plaza de la Cibeles** is splendid. The central fountain depicts Cybele, a controversial Greek fertility goddess, serenely settled in a chariot pulled by two lions. The sculptural ensemble is probably the best-known fountain in all Spain. The most unavoidable building on the plaza is the cathedral-like **Palacio de Comunicaciones**, teasingly nicknamed *Nuestra Señora de las Comunicaciones* (Our Lady of Communications). Inaugurated in 1919, the building is the quite remarkable central post office, with high ceilings and overhead walkways.

Also facing Plaza de la Cibeles, the **Banco de España** (Bank of Spain) headquarters combines Neo-classical, Baroque, and rococo styles. The financial district, Madrid's Wall Street, begins here on **calle de Alcalá**. Imposing buildings in this high-rent district contain the head offices or branches of more than 100 banks, plus insurance companies, the finance ministry, and on nearby Plaza de la Lealtad, the **Bolsa de Comercio** (Stock Exchange). Heading down leafy Paseo del Prado you'll find the first, and greatest, of the art museums here.

Behind the fountain at the Plaza de la Cibeles is the ornate and splendid central Spanish post office.

☛ Museo del Prado

Madrid's pride, the Prado museum, is indisputably the world's greatest collection of Spanish paintings and one of the world's most prestigious museums. Even apart from its Spanish treasures, it deserves high priority on any visitor's agenda for its hundreds of famous foreign works, especially of the Italian and Flemish schools. This immense hoard of art works, ranging from the 12th to the 19th century, was collected and donated by Spain's Hapsburg and Bourbon kings, private patrons of the arts, and convents and monasteries around the country.

Despite its greatness, the museum came about somewhat by chance. More than two centuries ago, Carlos III commissioned the architect Juan de Villanueva, draftsman of the royal palace,

to design this Neo-classical building. It was to have served as a museum of natural history, but after some eventful delays (Napoleon's invasion badly damaged the building), its mission was diverted to art, and the royal museum of painting was inaugurated in 1819. In 1868 it became *El Museo del Prado*.

In the early 1990s, modernization projects, such as desperately needed air condi-

Lines begin to form early in the day at the world renowned Prado museum.

tioning and humidity control, caused upheaval in the museum. Although these are now completed, further renovation and work on an extension are underway. The famed Spanish architect Rafael Moneo, a Pritzker prize winner, is set to begin the Prado's long-awaited expansion so that more of its vast collection can be exhibited.

The Prado owns perhaps 10,000 paintings, but at present can only display about 10 percent of them (the overflow is either in storage or on loan to museums around the world.) Seeing and appreciating even that many great paintings could

> Art lovers intent on seeing Madrid's Big Three art museums — the Prado, the Thyssen-Bornemisza, and the Reina Sofía — would do well to acquire the Paseo del Arte (Art Walk) voucher. It allows visits in all three museums for a single price: 1,275 ptas. (a considerable savings over the individual admission prices of each).

occupy a serious student of art for many weeks. Short-term visitors may have to settle for the condensed highlights, perhaps in a hectic couple of hours.

To take in more Old Masters per mile, it's vital to plan ahead. Decide what you want to see and head for it first, even if it demands that you rush past obvious masterworks. Given the usual crowds, you'd be wise to rest your feet from time to time, or seek refreshment in the basement restaurant.

Highlights of the Prado Museum

Spanish: Alongside modern master Pablo Picasso, **Diego Velázquez y Silva** (1599–1660) is the most famous Spanish painter who ever lived. He was hired by king Felipe IV and became an amazingly perceptive court painter and, quite simply, the greatest Spanish artist of the Golden Age. The royal family is featured in his seminal work, *Las Meninas* (the Maids of Honor). The artist painted himself with palette in hand at the left side of his own masterpiece, in a sense part of the family, as he became in real life.

Another vast, unforgettable Velázquez canvas here is *Surrender of Breda,* commemorating a Spanish victory over Dutch forces in 1625. The chivalry of the winning general, the exhaustion of the loser, the less disguised emotions of their retinues, the array of upraised lances, and the burning landscape communicated a profound pathos. Elsewhere are Velázquez's portraits of the high and the mighty, along with studies of fun-loving, ordinary mortals. Other great works include *Las Hilanderas* (The Spinners) and *Los Borrachos* (The Drunkards).

Francisco de Goya (1746–1828), another court painter, had a tumultuous, wildly varied career, and excellent selections from nearly every phase of it are collected in the Prado, which has the largest Goya ensemble in the world. A philanderer in his youth, Goya fled Zaragoza in 1763 for the anonymity of Madrid. He went on to become the king's principal artist. Of all the Prado's paintings, none is more discussed and disputed than *La Maja Desnuda* (The Naked Maja), one of Spain's first nudes. Rumors of a scandalous affair between Goya and the duchess of Alba have long been assumed. Goya's most celebrated royal portrait, *The Family of Carlos IV,* is daringly frank and unflattering; only the royal children look remotely attractive. On still another level, *The Executions of the 3rd of May,* one of history's most powerful protest pictures, depicts the shooting of Spanish patriots in 1808 by the French. Goya witnessed this tragedy of the War of Independence from his cottage, then went to the scene by moonlight to sketch the victims. New Goya rooms in the Prado were opened in March 1999. Goya's harrowing "black paintings," done when he was depressed and going deaf (see *Saturn Devouring One of His*

Goya's **Naked Maja** *occupies a central position among the many classic paintings on display at the Prado Museum.*

Sons) have been moved, temporarily, from the ground floor to the second floor. They will be a focal point of the Prado's planned expansion.

El Greco (1541–1614) was born in Crete and was long a resident in Italy, but nonetheless became a consummate Spanish painter. He worked in Toledo, his adopted city, for 37 years, toiling away at the immense and intensely personal religious canvases that are his hallmark. Asymmetrical compositions and a mystical mood of ecstasy typify his work. *Knight with his Hand on Chest,* an early portrait, is realistic and alive, a study of a deep-eyed, bearded *caballero* (gentleman) in black. It is signed, in Greek letters, "Domenikos Theotokopoulos," the artist's real name. The Prado is also well supplied with El Greco's passionately colored religious paintings, such as *Adoration of the Shepherds*.

Felipe II didn't care for El Greco's revolutionary style, and later critics wondered whether his elongated figures were the result of myopia, but his mystical masterpieces live on.

Francisco de Zurbarán (1598–1664), a member of the Seville school, combined mysticism and realism and was a master of light. His greatest works are of mythological, religious and historic themes. His deeply religious monks, priests, and saints are painted in flowing robes with almost tangible textures. The Prado owns his strained but fascinating battle picture, *The Defense of Cádiz against the English,* and the rarer *Still Life* of a goblet, two vases, and a pot emerging from a black background.

Bartolomé Murillo (1617–1682), Spain's most popular religious artist of his time, depicted revered Biblical personalities at ease. His tender scenes, as well as classical religious works with soaring angels, brought Murillo international fame, although detractors label his later work mawkish and saccharine.

José Ribera (c. 1591–1652) spent much of his life in Italy, where the Valencia-born artist was known as lo Spagnoletto (the little Spaniard). His portraits of saints, hermits, and martyrs reveal impeccable drawing skills, composition, and keen exploitation of light and shadow.

Dutch and Flemish: Hieronymus Bosch (c. 1450–1516), whom the Spanish call El Bosco, has three masterpieces in the Prado, including a large triptych called *The Garden of Earthly Delights.* Daringly mixing erotic fantasies and apocalyptic nightmares, it portrays the terrors and superstitions of the medieval peasant mind. Bosch's wild hallucinations presage similar psychological explorations 400 years later by Salvador Dalí.

Peter Paul Rubens (1577–1640), of noble ancestry, pursued a career as a diplomat as well as an artist. The prolific Rubens is represented by dozens of paintings in the Prado. Of particular note is the huge *Adoration of the Magi*, a brilliant religious extravaganza, and *The Three Graces,* a portrait of fleshy nudes with an equally lush landscape. The blonde on the left is said to be Rubens's second wife, Helena.

The greatest work of **Rogier van der Weyden** (c. 1400–1464), *Descent From the Cross,* an altarpiece, should not be missed.

Italian: Titian (c. 1490–1576) is represented by several paintings, one of the greatest of which is the *Portrait of the Emperor Carlos V.* Depicting Titian's patron in armor, on horseback at the battle of Mühlberg, it set the standard for court painters over the next century. Titian also produced religious works, but seemed to have no difficulty changing gears to the downright lascivious: *Baccanal* is about as far as an orgy can go within the bounds of a museum.

The collection of paintings by **Raphael** (1483–1520) in the Prado was once kidnapped by Napoleon and carted off to Paris, though soon recovered. Centuries of investigation

Disappearing Masters

Fate and turbulent times dealt unkindly with the last remains of Spain's three greatest painters.

El Greco died in Toledo in 1614. He was buried in a local church, but the coffin was transferred to another, which was destroyed. His bones were never found.

Velázquez (died in 1660) was entombed in a Madrid parish church, which was demolished in the early 19th century; the remains were lost. Finally, at the end of the 20th century, archaeologists claimed to have located his body, near the Royal Palace, 400 years after his birth.

Goya died in 1828 in Bordeaux, France, where he was interred. In 1899, the remains were sent back to Spain, but the skull was unaccountably missing.

have failed to uncover the identity of *The Cardinal,* Raphael's explosive character study of a subject with fishy eyes, aqualine nose, and cool, thin lips.

Tintoretto (1518–1594) brought mannerism to Venice. Look for his dramatic Bible stories, originally ceiling paintings, and, on quite another plane, the close-up of a *Lady Revealing her Bosom.* On your way through the Italian rooms, be sure to keep an eye peeled for **Fra Angelico**'s glowing and stupendous *Annunciation,* as well as for **Antonello da Messina**'s realistically detailed, intensely tragic *Christ Sustained by an Angel*, and **Sandro Botticelli**'s *The Story of Nastagio Degli Onesti.*

> Almost all of Madrid's museums are closed on Mondays and bank holidays. The exception is the Reina Sofía, which closes on Tuesdays. It is also open late — until 9pm every day but Sunday.

A Prado annex, the **Casón del Buen Retiro,** up the hill in calle de Felipe IV, houses a collection of 19th-century paintings, but remained closed for renovations in 2000.

Across the Paseo del Prado is the **Museo Thyssen-Bornemizsa,** a recent addition to Madrid's already impressive art collections housed in the Palacio de Villahermosa. This elegant three-story brick palace has been specifically renovated to house one of the largest known private collections of ancient and modern paintings, the property of the German industrialist Baron von Thyssen-Bornemizsa. More than 800 paintings are exhibited, dating from the 13th century to the present day. From the 19th and 20th centuries there are examples of trends such as the Paris school, German expressionism, Russian avant-garde, and American abstract painting. Like a survey of Western art, among the most important collections are classical works by Fra Angélico, Van Eyck, Dürer, Rembrandt, Hals, Titian, Van Dyck, and Rubens, and Impressionist works by Manet, Monet, Renoir,

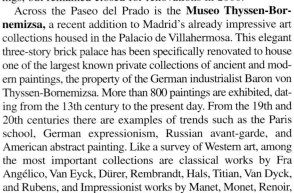

Gaugain, Toulouse-Lautrec, Cézanne, and Van Gogh, among many others. An impressive private collection it certainly is, but there are those who have criticized it as an ostentatious collection of minor works by major artists.

The third anchor in the golden art trio, a landmark of old Madrid, is the Hospital de San Carlos (c/ Santa Isabel 52), which now houses the **Centro de Arte Reina Sofía**. The museum focuses on Spanish and international 20th- century art, and is best known for exhibiting Picasso's monumental *Guernica* behind bulletproof glass.

A school trip to the Centro de Arte Reina Sofía, home of Picasso's **Guernica**.

Held in the Museum of Modern Art in New York until the death of Franco, per the artist's wishes, *Guernica,* a panorama of horror provoked by the Spanish Civil War bombing of a defenseless Basque town, is perhaps the 20th century's most famous painting. On display alongside are the original sketches and studies showing the work that went into the final canvas. The center also houses other paintings of Picasso, as well as an opulent collection of works by Miró, Dalí, Julio González, and Juan Gris.

Directly across from the Reina Sofía is the **Atocha train station,** an iron-and-glass affair with a small botanical garden inside. If you want to catch the high-speed AVE train to Córdoba and Seville, or other trains to the south of Spain, this is where you'll need to go. Southeast of the train station is the **Real Fábrica de Tapices** (Royal Tapestry Factory, c/ Fuenterrabía, 2). All that has changed since Felipe V founded this workshop in 1721 is the method of dyeing the wool. The same 18th-century looms are still used, though the number of workers has dwindled considerably. Goya worked here, creating the designs on which tapestries were based. They are still being copied, along with contemporary designs, on commission.

Immediately east of the Museo del Prado is the city's major green space, **Parque del Buen Retiro.** Until a little more than a century ago, Retiro Park was a royal preserve. Today its lawns, gardens and promenades are the most convenient and enjoyable place for many *Madrileños* to take a family outing (see page 9). In summer, kids and lovers rent

*The ornamental lake in the center of Retiro Park,
a spot popular with tourists as well as Madrileños.*

rowboats and paddle about the small lake in the center of the park. The **Palacio de Cristal** (Crystal Palace), a 19th-century iron and glass solarium that houses temporary art exhibitions, has finally reopened after years of renovations.

Another central breathing space, the **Real Jardín Botánico** (Royal Botanical Garden), adjacent to the Prado, was founded two centuries ago and is packed with enlightening displays of flowers and trees.

At the northwest corner of Retiro Park is **Puerta de Alcalá,** a monumental triumphal arch surmounted by warrior-angels, honoring Carlos III. Until the late 19th century, this marked the eastern edge of Madrid. Now the Plaza de la Independencia, in which the arch stands, is a bedlam of midtown traffic and gateway to newer barrios east.

MODERN MADRID

Madrid's third major expansion took place in the 19th century, resulting in the foundations of modern Madrid, a sprawling succession of residential neighborhoods, shops, cinemas, restaurants, banks and smaller museums. Barrio de Salamanca is the most attractive and exclusive of these, and Gran Vía is the great turn-of-the-century avenue that connects east to west, old to new Madrid.

Paseo de Recoletos is a continuation of Paseo del Prado that runs from Plaza de la Cibeles to Plaza Colón. A block east is the distinguished **Museo Arqueológico** (c/ Serrano, 13). The museum's archaeology collection addresses the art of ancient inhabitants of Spain, with statuettes and jewelry from 2nd-century B.C. Carthaginian settlers and miraculously preserved mosaics from 2nd-century A.D. Roman Spain. An unforgettable item is *La Dama de Elche* (the Lady of Elche), a stone sculpture found in Alicante province in 1897. This thoroughly noble goddess, with beautiful cheekbones, lips, and eyes, and wearing a fanciful headdress, may be 2,500 years old. On the museum grounds — or, more correctly, *under* the ground — is a careful reproduction of the painted scenes discovered in a cave in Altamira in northern Spain: prehistoric depictions of animals, dating back 15,000 years and representing man's first illustrations of the world around him. They are said to be some of the finest prehistoric cave drawings ever discovered.

> In many Madrid museums, the legends are in Spanish only. To decode placards, know that *siglo III A.C.* (antes de Cristo) = 3rd century B.C., while *siglo III D.C.* (después de Cristo) = 3rd century A.D.

Plaza de Colón is a large open space that has been the recent scene of far-reaching public-works projects. The city airport bus terminal operates below ground, beneath an 1885 statue of Christopher Columbus and a monument to the discovery of the New World. There is also the **Centro Cultural de la Villa** (City Cultural Center), with facilities for concerts, theatre, art exhibitions, and films.

Paseo de la Castellana is Madrid's principal north-south avenue, running for several miles through the heart of the city and bordering the Salamanca district to its west. In the area north of Plaza de Colón, you come to a newer section of town, where patrician townhouses in the central area give way to luxurious modern apartment blocks with landscaped balconies.

Museo Lázaro Galdiano (c/ Serrano, 122) is an astonishingly wide-ranging and priceless private collection. Featured here are ancient jewelry, including a Celtic diadem from the 2nd century B.C., medieval and Renaissance masterpieces in ivory and enamel, gold and silver, rare church vestments, and medieval weapons. Its paintings comprise a Rembrandt portrait of Saskia van Uylenburgh, dated the year they were married; Hieronymus Bosch at his most diabolical; a rich repository of Goya official portraits, colorful sketches of real life, and haunting scenes of witches and horrors; El Greco's sensitive *St. Francis of Assisi* and an early (1562) picture from his Venetian period; and the English painters Reynolds, Gainsborough, and Constable. But the museum's greatest pride, spotlighted in its own niche on the ground floor, is a portrait of angelic beauty, painted around 1480 by Leonardo Da Vinci, entitled *The Saviour*.

Another smaller but equally interesting museum is the **Museo Sorolla** (Paseo del General Martínez Campos, 37). The only Madrid museum devoted to a single painter, this mansion was the home and studio of Joaquín Sorolla (1863–1923). It has close to 300 paintings on view, showing the Valencian impressionist's favorite seaside scenes and landscapes. The house has a charming lived-in feel.

The Plaza de Toros Monumental de Las Ventas is the place to go to witness Spain's most famous sport, bullfighting.

Quite a way east of the Salamanca barrio is the **Plaza de Toros y Museo Taurino** (Bullfighting Ring and Museum), officially called the Plaza de Toros Monumental de Las Ventas. This is where to go to see an authentic bullfight, a seemingly anachronistic pursuit that continues to inspire the passions of so many Madrileños. The small museum houses historic posters, capes, swords, paintings, and photos for *aficionados* of the *corrida*, and is perhaps best visited out of bullfighting season for those who want to get a glimpse of the interior of the ring.

Gran Vía & Plaza de España

Bustling **Gran Vía** is a mix of hotels, shops, theatres, nightclubs, and cafés — the street for strolling and window-gazing. Connoisseurs of traffic jams will appreciate the nightmarish rush hour along this busy street. Pony-tailed policewomen frantically gesticulate and whistle in a doomed effort to stir the immovable traffic; drivers at their wit's end lean on their horns in sympathy and add to the cacophony. And a special bonus: In Madrid, thanks to the siesta lunch break, the rush hour happens not twice, but *three* times a day.

The avenue is a busy mix of architectural styles and contains several fine examples of Art Nouveau and Art Deco. Particularly noteworthy are the ornately French Edificio Metrópolis, at the junction of Alcalá, and the Palacio de la Música. From Plaza del Callao, the Gran Vía continues downhill towards the **Plaza de España** through more shopping, strolling, and nightlife territory. Two tall skyscrapers dominate the plaza. A favorite sight with visiting photographers is the Cervantes monument: A stone sculpture honoring the author looms behind bronze statues of his immortal characters, Don Quixote and Sancho Panza, astride their horse and donkey, respectively.

Museo Cerralbo (c/Ventura Rodríguez, 17), another nobleman's collection bequeathed to his country, is more like visiting an art collector's 19th-century house than a museum; few works are identified or marked. But there are paintings by El Greco, Murillo, Ribera, Zurbarán, Titian, and Caravaggio. The mansion's split-level library would make any bibliophile jealous.

In Parque del Oeste is a true curiosity, the **Templo Egipcio de Debod.** Threatened with submersion during the building of the Aswan high dam, this 25-century-old Egyptian temple was dis-

The ambiance of Gran Vía is defined by its buildings, which radiate a stately charm.

mantled and shipped to Madrid, stone by stone, as a gift to the Spanish government. The sight from the temple is also something special: a panoramic view over Madrid.

Calle de la Princesa, which begins at Plaza de España, is actually a northwest extension of the Gran Vía. The house at no. 22 is literally palatial, calling to mind a scaled-down Buckingham Palace. Tucked away in a comfortable park behind high railings, the **Palacio de Liria** is the residence of the duchess of Alba. The family picture gallery includes works by Rembrandt, Titian, Rubens, Van Dyck, El Greco, and Goya, but the palace is closed to the public except by special arrangement.

Calle de la Princesa's trajectory ends where the university district begins. The landmarks are the air force headquarters (a modern copy of El Escorial) and Madrid's youngest triumphal arch, which commemorates the Franco victory of 1939.

Aficionados of Spanish art and Goya in particular should not miss **La Ermita de San Antonio de la Florida** (Glorieta de San Antonio de la Florida, 5). In an area between the railway yards and the river, Goya's greatest frescoes, remarkably preserved, cover the cupola of an 18th-century chapel. The artist's tomb was installed in the church in 1919. An identical chapel was built alongside this one in 1929 so that Goya's frescoes and remains could rest in relative peace.

Ciudad Universitaria, the University City, was built on the ruins of the district that suffered the worst damage in the civil war. A drive around indicates the ambitious expanse of the campus and the mixture of architectural styles.

Sunday in Madrid

Sundays in some Spanish cities are sedate, with the streets enervated of life. Not Madrid. Check out these lively scenes:

The Rastro. On Sunday mornings, the streets of Old Madrid, beginning just south of the cathedral, are transformed into one of the world's biggest flea markets. Tens of thousands of bargain-minded Madrileños join the out-of-towners in pricing clothing, antiques, pots and pans, and junk of all sorts.

The Stamp Market. Hundreds of collectors assemble in the Plaza Mayor on Sunday mornings to buy and sell stamps, coins, banknotes, cigar bands, and even used lottery tickets. Watch the enthusiasts with their tweezers and magnifying glasses.

The Book Fair. Just south of the Botanical Garden, the bibliophiles throng to open-air stalls along calle de Claudio Moyano. New and used books bought and sold: trash, comics, foreign fiction and valuable old tomes.

Museo de América (Av. de los Reyes Católicos, 6; in Ciudad Universitaria) is a superb collection of art and artifacts from América, which in Spain means Central and South America. There are pre-Columbian pieces from Peru and Mexico, including two rare Mayan manuscripts (códices), replete with the mysterious symbols and delightful illustrations that have long fascinated scholars.

Parque Casa de Campo is another former royal preserve, forested by Felipe II in 1559. It can be reached by bus, suburban railway line, or cable car *(teleférico)*. Thousands of acres of woodland are interspersed with attractions and amenities. Visitors can hire a boat on the park lake, swim in the pool, or check out the zoo (built in 1972), where 150 kinds of animals pace back and forth behind moats, not bars.

EXCURSIONS FROM MADRID

Toledo

Pop. 65,000 (70 km/43 miles southwest of Madrid)

If you make only a single side trip from Madrid, the legendary city of Toledo, home to El Greco and a Middle Ages

These handsome tiles depict an archetypal Spanish pattern, decorating the courtyard at the Alcázar in Toledo.

The Toledo skyline at sunset shows off a city that in spirit still evokes the Middle Ages.

melting pot of diverse cultures, should be the one. A survey of the history of Spain — its tradition, grandeur, art, architecture and mix of cultures — is crammed into this small city on a Castilian hilltop. The one-time imperial capital remains the religious center of Spain and an incomparable treasure-trove of fine arts. You are more than likely to get lost exploring the tiny back streets, little changed since the 16th century, but you'll never forget the adventure.

Successively conquered by the Romans and Visigoths, Toledo became the capital of Spain in 1085. Until the Christian Reconquest, Toledo was a place of religious and cultural harmony. Even though the Moors and Jews were expelled from the city, Toledo remains alive with their remarkable contributions. The city is a fascinating and congested labyrinth of churches, synagogues, mosques, noble houses and humble residences.

The **Catedral de Toledo,** right in the center of the old town, is one of Spain's most recognized and spectacular sights — it is visible from any part of town, thanks to its Gothic tower topped by a spire ringed by spikes. At ground level, the asymmetrical cathedral is hemmed in by Toledo's clutter of back streets, making it difficult to position yourself for a sufficiently dramatic view. Even so, its abundant glory is immediately apprehended inside — the stained glass, wrought iron, sculpture, and paintings are by a stable of many of Spain's greatest geniuses.

> Toledo is the most popular day trip in Spain, and in high season the small city is overrun with tour buses and groups. To savor atmospheric Toledo as it was, and can still be, it's best to plan an overnight stay.

Toledo's eminence as the center of Christian Spain dates to the first synods and ecclesiastical councils held there as early as the year 400. But with the Muslim invasion of Spain in 711, Christianity went underground. After the Reconquest of Toledo in 1085, with the legendary warrior El Cid leading the way, mosques were converted into churches. In 1222, funds were appropriated for a fitting cathedral. The construction lasted two and a half centuries; the ornamentation took considerably longer.

In the center of the five-aisled Gothic basilica, the **Coro** (choir) is a marvel of woodcarving. Illustrations of the Christian triumph at Granada in 1492, on the lower choir stalls, were created by Rodrigo Alemán only three years after the great event itself. The higher stalls came later, carved by the Renaissance masters Alonso Berruguete and Felipe Bigarny. The 13th- or 14th-century smiling statue known as *The White Virgin* is believed to be French.

The ornate entrance to the Puerta de Los Leones is a prelude to the grand cathedral.

Across the transept, though, the **main altar** outdoes the coro's splendor. A magnificent polychrome *retablo,* rising in five tiers, depicts New Testament stories in fervent detail. Just behind the back wall of the main chapel, the *Transparente* is the cathedral's most unforgettable innovation. The fantastically elaborate work is by one man, Narciso Tomé, architect, sculptor, and painter. The 18th-century artist opened the cathedral's ceiling to draw light into the sanctuary, at the same time leading the eyes of worshippers heavenwards. The cathedral's 750 stained-glass windows are sublimely restrained, but Tomé's bronze, marble, and jasper ensemble of color, shape, and symbolism is startling, and, daring as it is, much criticized.

The **Sala Capitular** (Chapter House) is a strangely oriental room with an intricate ceiling in the style called *mudéjar* (the work of Muslims performed for Christians after the Reconquest). On the walls are portraits of the archbishops of Toledo, beginning with St. Eugene (A.D. 96) and including Cardinal Cisneros, who ordered the construction of this hall.

In the **Tesoro** (Treasury), reliquaries, chalices, and crowns take a back seat to the lavish 16th-century monstrance (also ordered by Cisneros). This towering vessel, comprising 5,600 individual parts and subsequently gilded, was the work of the German silversmith Heinrich von Harff. Precious stones add to the glitter. The monstrance is said to weigh 17 *arrobas* (over 440 pounds).

The **Sacristía** (Sacristy) is an art museum within the cathedral. There are 16 El Grecos in this small collection. In addition to portraits of the virgin, Christ on the cross, and the apostles, there is a large and outstanding El Greco work over the main altar of the sacristy — *Expolio* (*The Denuding of Christ*). The sacristy also displays first-rate paintings by Goya, Titian, and Velázquez.

The cathedral's only competitor for domination of the Toledo skyline is the **Alcázar,** a fortress destroyed and rebuilt many times. It began as a Roman redoubt, but its present style was devised in the 16th century. Since then it has been used as a royal palace, army post, school, and prison.

Spanish Dramatists

Spain's three top dramatists of the Golden Age were prolific enough to make many celebrated writers seem dawdlers in contrast.

Lope de Vega (1562–1635) devised a new three-act format and turned out some 1,500 plays.

Tirso de Molina (c 1571–1648) wrote more than 300 plays, including the first about the world's most famous lover, Don Juan.

Pedro Calderón de la Barca (1600–1681) is credited with more than 100 comedies, tragedies, and religious allegories.

Madrileños all three, these men had checkered careers. Lope de Vega joined the Armada. Tirso de Molina served as a monk on the island of Santo Domingo. Calderón enlisted as a cavalry man and was later ordained a priest.

During the Spanish Civil War, it was a stronghold of the pro-Franco forces, who held out during a 72-day siege that all but destroyed it. The nationalist commandant, Colonel José Moscardó Ituarte, received a telephone call from the enemy announcing that his son, held hostage, would be executed unless the fortress surrendered. In a supremely Spanish reply, the colonel advised his son to "pray, shout 'Viva España' and die like a hero." More than a month after the son was killed, the siege was lifted. The citadel now holds an only moderately interesting military museum.

The triangular-shaped main plaza of Toledo has also been rebuilt after civil war destruction. The **Plaza de Zocodover** is where the Moorish market (zoco) was held in the Middle Ages. It was also the scene of the great fiestas, tournaments, and executions of criminals and infidels. Suggestively, the

A group of museum-goers gaze at the works of El Greco, an artist commonly associated with Toledo.

horseshoe arch leading from the square towards the river is called El Arco de Sangre (Arch of Blood).

Just down the hill beyond the arch, on calle de Cervantes, the **Museo de Santa Cruz** (Museum of the Holy Cross) is

housed in the sumptuous 16th-century Hospital of the Holy Cross, as notable as the contents within. The main portal is of stone carved in the style called plateresque, because it seems as delicate as a silversmith's work

> El Greco painted himself into the *Burial of the Count of Orgaz* — he's the seventh figure from the left at the bottom, staring straight ahead.

(*platero* means silversmith). Inside, great wooden ceilings add to a feeling of opulent spaciousness. The provincial archaeological museum is housed here, but greater interest accrues to the art collection. El Greco fans are in for a happy surprise — a wide selection of his works, highlighted by the *La Asunción de la Virgen,* painted just a year before the artist's death. Throughout the building are superb 16th-century tapestries, furniture and decorative arts.

The parish church **Iglesia de Santo Tomé** is a landmark because of its stately *mudéjar* tower. But visitors crowd into a small annex of the church with one intent: to view a single painting, one of Spain's supreme masterpieces, El Greco's *Burial of the Count of Orgaz.* The spectacular, large canvas, the single most famous image of Toledo, fuses the mundane and the spiritual, depicting grave-faced local noblemen attending the count's funeral. Tradition says two saints made an appearance at the funeral. El Greco shows St. Augustine and St. Stephen, in splendid ecclesiastical garb, lifting the count's body. Above, angels and saints crowd the clouds. The whole story is told in perfect pictorial balance, and with El Greco's penchant for long, heaven-gazing faces and characteristic colors.

El Greco spent the most productive years of his prolific career in Toledo. Just down the hill from Santo Tomé, the **Casa-Museo El Greco** — misleadingly named, since the artist almost certainly never lived in it — has been reconstructed and linked to a museum dedicated to his life. Still, it has authentic 16th-century furnishings and a tranquil garden that at the least replicate the look and feel of a Toledan house of the era. Several of the master's paintings are on display, among them *A View of Toledo* and *Portrait of St. Peter*. The **El Greco house** was originally built by Samuel Levi, a 14th-century Jewish financier and friend of King Peter I of Castile.

From the 12th to the 16th centuries, Toledo was a center of Jewish poets, historians, and philosophers. Jews, Moors, and Benedictine monks worked alongside each other in translation teams. As Europe awakened from the Dark Ages, Toledo provided a key link in transmitting vital knowledge of Arabic science and Greek philosophy to the Western world.

During those halcyon days, Samuel Levi, as devout as he was rich, built a synagogue next to his home, **Sinagoga del Tránsito** (Synagogue of the Dormition). Muslim artists created a ceiling of cedar imported from Lebanon; they adorned the walls with filigrees of impressive intricacy, as well as inscriptions in Hebrew from the psalms. Upstairs, a large gallery was reserved for the women of the congregation. Curiously, Christian tombstones are found in the floor; after the expulsion of the Jews from Spain, the synagogue was converted into a church. Today the **Museo Sefardí** (Sephardic Museum) is attached to Samuel Levi's synagogue, with exhibits of medieval tombs, scrolls, and vestments.

Like the Tránsito, **Sinagoga de Santa María la Blanca** (Synagogue of St. Mary the White) received its present name after being converted to a church. No signs of the Jewish presence remain, yet this five-aisled building, with 24 columns supporting horse-shoe arches, was the main synagogue of 12th-century Toledo. Much more apparent is its Muslim connection; the building was constructed by Moorish artisans and looks much more like a mosque than a synagogue or church. In the 15th century, blood-thirsty mobs raided the syna-gogue and massacred the Jewish population. After the pogrom, the old structure served a bizarre variety of purposes — as a Catholic chapel, a convent for "fallen" women, army barracks, and quartermaster's depot. Even empty, as it is now, it still evokes dramatic memories.

The cloisters of the Monasterio de San Juan de los Reyes is not to be missed.

Monasterio de San Juan de los Reyes (Monastery of St. John of the Kings), built by the Catholic monarchs Ferdinand and Isabella from their private fortune, in commemoration of the 1476 victory over the Portuguese in the battle of Toro. *mudéjar* elements, it maintains a poignant souvenir on the outer wall — the chains that held Christian prisoners of the Moors. The spectacular cloister is a superb example of mostly late-Gothic style, with elaborate stone carvings.

The main entrance into Toledo, between the "new" 16th-century gateway **Puerta Nueva de Bisagra** and the bullring, stands the **Hospital de Tavera** — equal parts palace, orphanage, and church — built by a 16th-century archbishop of Toledo, Juan Pardo de Tavera. The library contains fascinating old manuscripts as well as the bound volumes of the hospital's financial accounts, which record expenditures in a meticulous script. In the dining room hangs a portrait by Titian of the Emperor Carlos V and a painting of the princess Clara Eugenia by Claudio Coello. El Greco is also strongly represented elsewhere in the palace. His portrait of the Virgin is stirringly beautiful, while *Baptism of Christ* is one of the artist's last works. A curiosity here is Ribera's portrait of a bearded woman. Notice the small statue of Christ resurrected, an experiment in sculpture by El Greco.

A fine view of Toledo — still very similar to the one painted by El Greco of his beloved city — can be had just across the river, north of the city. By car, the drive along the Carretera de Circunvalación, the beltway that parallels the River Tagus around the city, leads towards Parador hotel and the Roman bridge, Puente de Alcántara. The views are stupendous, especially at sunset. Visitors without access to an automobile seeking a similar view should walk out through

---

A Madrileño Lexicon

Tasca. A bar specializing in tapas, tasty snacks consumed while standing in a litter of prawn shells and olive stones.

Tertulia. The unofficial club of conversationalists meeting in a café. The tradition is withering as the pace of life in the capital accelerates.

Tuna. Band of troubadours in medieval costume, usually university students, who serenade clients in bars and restaurants for tips.

Zarzuela. A uniquely Spanish form of operetta, often on themes indigenous to Madrid.

---

the San Martín neighborhood, west of the old Jewish quarter, over the San Martín bridge (which dates to 1203), behind which Toledo rises dramatically on the hill.

If you're driving back to Madrid from Toledo and want to make a brief stop almost exactly mid-way, the village of **Illescas** (33 km/20 miles from Toledo) holds a surprise, especially for art aficionados. Its **Hospital de la Virgen de la Caridad** (Convent of the Virgin of Charity), has five El Grecos hanging in its church.

Aranjuez and Chinchón

Aranjuez

Pop. 39,000 (50 km/30 miles. south of Madrid)

The deep-green water of the Río Tajo, reflecting the noble buildings of Aranjuez, nourishes parks and formal gardens, as well as the prized local crops of asparagus and strawberries. The town can be reached by the picturesque "Strawberry Train" (Tren de la Fresa), which leaves Atocha station at 10am on weekends, returning in the early evening, from April through July, and September.

As you cross the bridge into Aranjuez on the road from Madrid, the spacious, geometric town plan becomes apparent. The balanced main square — actually a huge rectangle — is faced by arcaded buildings on two sides and the church of St. Anthony at the south end. But here the civic sights take second place to the royal parks and palaces. Ever since Ferdinand and Isabella, Spanish monarchs have retreated to this oasis to escape Madrid's summer heat. Since the 18th century, they've enjoyed the luxury of a first-class country palace reminiscent of Versailles. In the mid-19th century, a railway line ran into the **Palacio Real** (Royal Palace) to the foot of the staircase.

Guided tours of the palace cover 22 rooms, enough to reveal a cross-section of royal taste in furniture, paintings, sculpture, tapestries, clocks, pianos, music-boxes, and bric-a-brac. The **Porcelain Room** contains decorations created by the Buen Retiro porcelain factory of Madrid for king Carlos III in 1760. The walls are covered with porcelain figures telling exotic stories: a Japanese samurai, Chinese mandarins, monkeys, and birds. Seven mirrors, a weird porcelain chandelier, a circular couch, and a fine marble floor complete the dazzling design. In the **Smoking Room**, based on the hall of the two sisters in the Alhambra at Granada, red damask couches sprawl along the walls of this mid-19th-century reproduction. The **Chinese painting salon** holds 200 ingenious rice-paper paintings, gifts from a Chinese emperor in the mid-19th century.

A combined ticket covers all the sights in the palaces, gardens, and museums. Less than 2 km (about a mile) from the royal palace, the curiously named **farmer's cottage** *(la casita del labrador)* is set in the extensive prince's garden. Far from being a cottage, this is a condensed palace to which the kings retreated for parties and hunting weekends.

Busts of ancient philosophers give the **statue gallery** its name, but the big attraction is what first seems to be a far-fetched fountain in the center of the room. It turns out instead to be a far-fetched clock, an 1850 folly, incorporating simulated water jets and a large music box. This being an informal palace, the **Ballroom** is barely large enough to accommodate 200 noble dancers. The **Platinum Room,** as sumptuous as it sounds, leads to the king's own toilet, wittily arranged as a plush throne.

Elsewhere in the prince's garden, in a modern building called the **Sailor's House** *(Casa de Marinos),* you can find out what became of the quaint "Tagus squadron" of the royal fleet. The kings of Spain enjoyed being rowed down the river in gala launches. These flagships are preserved in the Sailor's House, along with related nautical mementoes.

Aside from the palaces and museums, Aranjuez is noted for its royal parks and gardens. The formal gardens are a wonder of flowers, clipped hedges, sculptures, and fountains.

Chinchón

A nice side trip (20 km or 12 miles) from Aranjuez, through gently undulating hill country, leads to Chinchón. Here is charming proof that you do not have to travel hundreds of

Chinchón is immersed in old-world flavor, as exemplified by this baker's shop.

miles from Madrid to immerse yourself in the Spain of pack-donkeys on cobbled lanes. The town square could be a stage set: Two- and three-story white stucco houses with wooden arcades surround an irregular, but vaguely oval plaza.

Chinchón is celebrated as the home of various aniseed liqueurs. It also grows a much-vaunted species of garlic, sold locally in strung bouquets.

El Escorial

(49 km/30 miles west of Madrid)

More than a mere palace, El Escorial is an entire royal city — living quarters, church, monastery, mausoleum, and museum — under one roof. In a distinctly Spanish version of Italian Renaissance style, it depicts the physical and spiritual superlatives of the empire's Golden Age.

King Felipe II ordered El Escorial built in celebration of Spain's victory over French forces in 1557 at the battle of St. Quentin, in France. The king himself died here in 1598, to be buried in a family tomb beneath the high altar of the basilica. Sheer statistics don't do full justice to the extravagant scale of the royal palace complex, built in only 21 years. The longest wall is more than 295 meters (970 feet) from corner tower to tower. The dome of the palace church rises 92 meters (302 feet). By official count, the building contains 43 altars, 86 stairways, more than 1,200 doors, and 2,600 windows. Spaniards used to call it the eighth wonder of the world.

Juan de Herrera, considered the greatest Spanish architect of the age, inherited the project after another architect had only begun the work. He also built the royal palace of Aranjuez and reconstructed the Alcázar of Toledo.

The mood achieved by the **Basílica**, shaped like a Greek cross, is one of devout magnificence. The immense main retable is composed of red marble, green jasper, and gilded bronze. The 124 finely carved seats in the choir include a slightly roomier one for Felipe II. Of the dozens of artworks collected here, none attracts more admiration than the life-size marble crucifix by Benvenuto Cellini of Florence. It is said that the great Renaissance artist originally planned the statue to adorn his own grave.

Exactly below the high altar, at the bottom of a flight of marble stairs, the **Panteón Real** (Royal Pantheon) is a subterranean churchyard of history. In the central hall, identical marble sarcophagi are stacked four high. Gilded angels hold lamps illuminating the terse Latin inscriptions. Of all the Hapsburg and Bourbon kings who ruled Spain, only two are

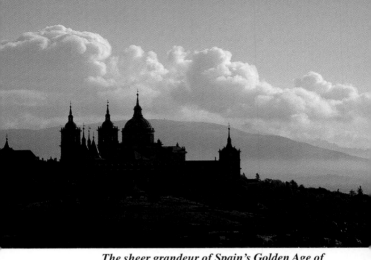

The sheer grandeur of Spain's Golden Age of architecture elevates El Escorial from its surroundings.

missing (Felipe V is buried at La Granja de San Ildefonso, Ferdinand VI in Madrid). Adjoining chambers are assigned to lesser royal personages, with a gloomy area devoted to the princes who died in childhood.

Above ground again, 40,000 rare books and manuscripts of immeasurable beauty and value are preserved in the **biblioteca** (library) created by Felipe II. Architect Herrera even took pains to design the bookcases, done in rare woods. The vaulted ceiling is a sight in itself — a painting symbolizing the arts and sciences, specifically grammar, rhetoric, dialectic, arithmetic, music, geometry, and astronomy. At opposite ends, philosophy and theology are extolled.

After seeing the church, mausoleum, and library, visitors are shown through the **Palacio de los Borbones** (Palace of the Bourbons). One room is more lavish than the next. The tapestries based on original designs by Goya and Rubens are outstanding. On the opposite side of the courtyard of the masks (named after the design of two fountains), the **Salones Reales** (apartments of Felipe II) are modest in comforts, but rich in artworks. The king died here among cherished paintings—a fantastic triptych by Hieronymus Bosch and works on religious themes by German, Flemish, and Italian artists.

In addition to the fine paintings found elsewhere in the escorial, the **new museums** have been created to display the great works commissioned or collected by the Spanish monarchs. In the stately surroundings hang pictures by Bosch, Ribera, Tintoretto, and Velázquez. El Greco enthusiasts will

find half a dozen of his canvases, including a unique portrait of Felipe II at prayer in a sweeping celestial scene, as well as the classic *Martirio de San Mauricio* (The Martyrdom of St. Maurice), full of sensitive detail.

Valle de los Caídos
(58 km/36 miles northwest of Madrid)

In a forested valley in the center of Spain, Francisco Franco decreed that a memorial for

Valle de los Caídos — a memorial for the victims of the Spanish Civil War.

the victims of the Civil War be built on a site chosen personally by him. The monument is at least equally dedicated to the Fascist dictator.

Thirty-five years later, in 1975, the *caudillo* (strongman) was buried beneath a simple stone slab in the monumental church of the Valley of the Fallen. Officially, it is termed the "largest basilica ever built in the history of mankind." The colossal monument was hewn out of the side of the mountain like a railway tunnel. The stone cross marking the basilica rises 150 meters (492 feet) from its base on top of a rocky outcrop. The cross is said to weigh 181,740 tons. The arcaded façade of the church, in a style reminiscent of Italian fascist architecture, is big enough to fill one side of the esplanade.

Segovia

Pop. 54,000 (88 km/55 miles northwest of Madrid)

Charming Segovia is yet another Castilian city that looks like a movie set: Its dramatic outline rises up majestically from the surrounding plains. The city's setting is picturesque Castilian *campo* — wide-open space interrupted only by a clump of trees, a lonely farmhouse, or an occasional a monastery or castle. The Sierra de Guadarrama fills half the horizon.

Segovia is a city of great historical monuments, all testament to Spain's one-time glories: a 2,000-year-old aqueduct, a storybook Alcázar, and one of Spain's finest cathedrals.

The wondrous **Roman Aqueduct,** a work of art and a triumph of engineering, marches right through the center of town. The aqueduct is composed of thousands of granite blocks arranged in graceful arches, sometimes two-tiered, but without mortar or cement of any kind. It is nearly a kilometer (half-mile) long, and it rises to a height of 46 meters (150 feet). This is the last lap of a conduit bringing water from a mountain stream to the walled city. The aqueduct was

Segovia's aqueduct, built by the Romans, was only recently put out of commission after nearly 2,000 years.

in constant use for 100 generations, with only a couple of details changed. A modern pipeline has been installed in the channel atop the aqueduct, and in the 16th century, a statue of Hercules in a niche over the tallest arch was replaced by a Christian image. Traffic was only recently diverted from passing through the aqueduct's arches, as pollution was threatening permanent damage to the irreplaceable structure.

The fairytale **Alcázar,** Segovia's incomparable royal castle, was erected in a strategic spot, on a ridge overlooking the confluence of two rivers, with an unimpeded view of the plateau in all directions. The Romans are thought to have been among the first to build a watchtower here. The present castle, reportedly the model for Disneyland, is a far cry from the simple stone fortress that took shape in the 12th century.

As the fortress grew bigger and more luxurious, it played a more significant historical role. By the 13th century, parliaments were convened here. In 1474, princess Isabella stayed in the Alcázar at the time of her coronation as queen of Castile, and in 1570, King Felipe II married his fourth bride, Anna of Austria, at the citadel. Less ceremoniously, the tower of King Juan II became a dungeon for 16th-century political prisoners. The most fanciful and photogenic parts of the castle's superstructure — its feast of turrets and towers — are the work of restoration after a disastrous fire in 1862. From the top of a hefty climb up the tower are breathtaking views of Segovia and the valley beyond.

From whatever part of town you view it, the **Catedral** is a beautiful sight. Its pinnacles, buttresses, and cupolas seem to belong to a whole complex of churches, not a single elegant monument. Begun in 1525 (but not consecrated until 1768), this is the last of the great Spanish Gothic cathedrals and possibly the last Gothic church in Europe. Its grace and style have won it the nickname of "grand dame of cathedrals." Incidentally, the cathedral was even taller until a lightning bolt lopped off the main tower in 1614. The reconstruction plan warily lowered the profile by more than 10 percent.

Inside, the cathedral's majestic columns and arches are lit by fine stained-glass windows. Two 18th-century organs are spectacularly flamboyant. Less obvious are the altarpieces in the chapels, the most important element of which (just to the right of the entrance) is a 16th-century polychrome *Pietà* by the Valencian Juan de Juni.

Delicate arches line the cloister, which belonged to the former cathedral that was destroyed; it was moved here, stone by stone, in the 16th century and put back together. The adjacent museum and chapter house contain a number of interesting pieces of religious art and relics, including

17th-century tapestries, the Baroque carriage propelled through the streets of Segovia every Corpus Christi, and the reminder of a 14th-century tragedy: the tomb of the infant prince Pedro, son of Enrique II. He slipped from the arms of his nurse as she admired the view from an open window of the Alcázar. The nanny scarcely hesitated before she leaped after him to her death in the moat below.

The main square of Segovia, the **Plaza Mayor,** combines history with real-life bustle. Buildings as pleasing as the 17th-century town hall face the large oblong plaza where shoppers, businessmen, and tourists take time out for coffee in the fresh air. During festivals, the square springs to life with excitement and color.

Only a few streets away to the east, a much older church than the cathedral graces Segovia's most charming square. **La Iglesia de St. Martín** is a 12th-century Romanesque beauty with glorious portals and porches. Plaza de San Martín, which slopes down to calle de Juan Bravo, is surrounded by noble mansions.

Next to the church, the prison-like building with those fierce, barred windows was, in fact, a prison when it was built in the 17th century. Now it houses a library and archives. Here and throughout the city, the façades of buildings are subject to elaborate three-dimensional decoration,

Don't be surprised if this Alcázar is reminiscent of the castle at Disneyland.

mainly with geometric forms. The most unique example, the nearby **Casa de los Picos,** bristles with pointed protuberances.

Total tranquility permeates the **Monasterio de El Parral**, founded in the mid-15th century just beyond the city walls (but within easy reach of the center of town). The architectural details, including a Gothic cloister, are being restored in fits and starts. Especially dramatic is the 16th-century high retable in the monastery's church.

Even more interesting, also just outside the wall and almost in the shadow of the Alcázar, is the **Iglesia de la Vera Cruz**, an unusual 12-sided structure dating from the early 13th century. The knights of the Holy Sepulchre held court in its unique double-decker chapel surrounded by a circular nave. The Maltese order, owner of the church for centuries, renovated it in the 1950s.

So much of Segovia is superlative that the 11th-century city wall itself is almost relegated to second-class status. A walk around the 2 ½ km (1 ½ miles) of wall is irregular but evocative.

La Granja de San Ildefonso, about 10 km (6 miles) southeast of Segovia (80 km or 50 miles north of Madrid), is a huge palace set in classic formal gardens. Here, too, the tapestries, 16th- to 18th-century masterpieces, are well worth seeing; they were collected by the Spanish royal family.

Riofrío, about 10 km (6 miles) south of Segovia (85 km or 53 miles north of Madrid), has an 18th-century palace that is quite modest compared to other palaces of Castile. Part of it is now devoted to the **Museo de Caza** (Hunting Museum), with stuffed animals and ancient weapons. The palace is reached by taking the scenic road through the deer sanctuary.

Ávila

Pop. 38,200 (112 km/70 miles northwest of Madrid)

The fairy-tale stone walls (*murallas*) protecting Ávila, one of the great images of medieval Spain, are rather too perfect:

from afar, they make the city look like a Castilian Disneyland. But they were built in all seriousness in the last decade of the 11th century. The ramparts are arguably Europe's finest extant fortifications, and they are the undisputed highlight of Ávila. They measure 2 1/2 km (1 1/2 miles) long, averaging 12 meters (40 feet) in height, with 88 towers and an estimated 2,500 niches suitable for sentries or marksmen.

If you're visiting Madrid in summer, you'll appreciate the cooler mountain air of Ávila — Spain's highest provincial capital, at more than 1,125 meters (3,700 feet) above sea level. Before the "modern" Ávila was built behind its crenellated wall, Celtiberians settled in the area and are credited with having sculpted the crude stone statues of bulls and pigs around the city.

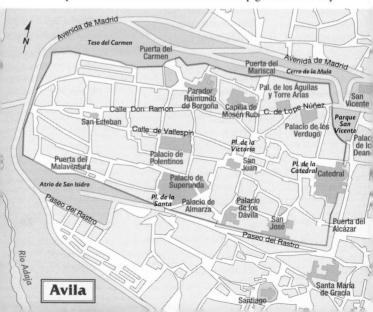

Besides its walls, Ávila is famous for its long association with Santa Teresa de Ávila — the mystic and church reformer St. Theresa. Born in Ávila in 1515, she spent three decades in the **Convento de la Incarnación,** outside the city walls, as a novice and later as prioress. The **Convento de Santa Teresa** was built on the site of the saint's birthplace. Among the other landmarks, the **Convento de San José** was founded by St. Theresa in 1562, the first of 17 Carmelite convents she eventually established. Theresa was canonized in 1622 and proclaimed a doctor of the church in 1970. In Ávila, you can see relics and manuscripts and even the habit St. Theresa wore in a remarkable life of prayer, penance, and poverty.

The **Catedral,** built between the 12th and 16th centuries, includes Romanesque, Gothic, and Renaissance elements. It even has a fortified head (cimorro) that is part of the city walls. Fine stained-glass windows accentuate the grace of the interior. The choir stalls, carved to illustrate the lives of the saints, are attributed to the 16th-century Dutch master known as Cornelius de Holanda. The high retable was begun by Pedro Berruguete, Spain's first great Renaissance artist, but he died in 1504, before it could be finished. In the ambulatory behind the altar is a brilliantly sculpted alabaster monument, the tomb of bishop Alonso de Madrigal, whose dark complexion won him the nickname *el tostado* (the toasted one).

The **Basílica de San Vicente** just outside the city walls is considerably smaller than the cathedral, but hardly less inspiring. The main (west) portico features lifelike statues of the apostles — barefoot, long-haired, bearded men, seemingly caught off guard by a candid sculptor. Inside, an extraordinary tomb commemorates San Vincente of Zaragoza and his two sisters, martyred in the 4th century. Knights of old placed their hands on this 12th-century sepulchre when they took their oaths.

Melancholy history surrounds the **Monasterio de San Tomás** (to the southeast, down the hill), the construction of which was sponsored by Ferdinand and Isabella. Their only son, prince Don Juan, died here at the age of 19, and his tomb lies in the monastery. It's worth climbing the old stone stairs to the choir loft to see the wood-carvings, particularly on the seats reserved for the Catholic monarchs themselves. This was also the head-quarters of the monarchs' confessor and adviser, the noted friar Tomás de Torquemada. As the first grand inquisitor of Spain, he was the enthusiastic leader of the 15th-century witch-hunt.

After you've seen Ávila up close — the cobbled streets, the mansions, the storks' nests in the belfries — drive or take a bus across the River Adaja to the monument called **Cuatro Postes** (Four Posts). The simple columned structure — marking the spot where Theresa fled as a youngster already consumed with religious visions — is secondary to the location. From this rocky hill you look back on the entire panorama of medieval Ávila.

Ávila's city walls, among the world's most finely crafted extant fortifications, were originally built in the 11th century.

Selected Hours and Admissions
Old Madrid
Ermita de San Antonio de la Florida. Glorieta de la Florida, 5. Tel. 91/542 07 22. Tuesdays–Friday, 10am–2pm and 4pm–8pm; Saturday and Sunday and holidays, 10am–2pm. 300 ptas. (Wednesdays free admission)

Monasterio de las Descalzas Reales. Plaza de las Descalzas, s/n. Tel. 91/542 00 59. Tuesday, Wednesday, Thursday and Saturday, 10:30am–12:45pm and 4pm–5:45pm; Friday, 10:30am–12:45pm; Sunday and holidays, 11am–1:45pm. 650 ptas. (Wednesday free admission for EU members; joint admission with Monasterio de la Encarnación, 825 ptas.)

Monasterio de la Encarnación. Plaza de la Encarnación, s/n. Tel. 91/542 00 59. Tuesday, Wednesday, Thursday and Saturday, 10:30am–12:45pm and 4pm–5:45pm; Friday, 10:30 am–12:45pm; Sunday and holidays, 11am–1:45pm. 425 ptas. (Wednesday free admission for EU members; joint admission with Monasterio de las Descalzas Reales, 825 ptas.)

Palacio Real. C/ Bailén, s/n. Tel. 91/547 53 50. Monday–Saturday, 9:30am–5:30pm, Sunday and holidays, 9:30am–2:30pm. 850 ptas. (guided tour, 950 ptas.)

Bourbon Madrid
Museo del Prado. Edificio Juan de Villanueva/Paseo del Prado, s/n. Tel. 91/330 29 00 <www.museoprado.mcu.es> Tuesday–Sunday, 9am–7pm; Sunday and holidays, 9am–2pm. 500 Ptas.

Museo Nacional Centro de Arte Reina Sofía. C/ Santa Isabel, 52 (at Paseo del Prado). Tel. 91/467 50 62. Monday–Saturday, 10am–9pm; Sunday and holidays, 10am– 2:30pm. 500 ptas.

Museo Thyssen-Bornemizsa. Paseo del Prado, 8. Tel. 91/369 01 51. Tuesday–Sunday, 10am–7pm. 700 ptas.

Salamanca & Beyond
Museo Lázaro Galdiano. C/ Serrano, 122. Tel. 91/561 60 84. Tuesday–Sunday, 10am–2pm. 500 ptas. (Wednesdays free admission)

Museo Sorolla. Gral. Martínez. Campos, 37. Tel. 91/310 15 84. Tuesday–Saturday, 10am–3pm; Sunday and holidays, 10am–2pm. 500 ptas.

El Escorial
Real Monasterio de San Lorenzo de El Escorial. Oct–Mar, Tuesday–Sunday 10am–5pm; Apr–Sept, 10am–6pm 10am–6pm. 850 pta.

Toledo
Alcázar. C/ General Moscardó, 4. Tel. 925/22 30 38. Tuesday–Sunday, 9:30am–2pm. 200 ptas.

Cathedral de Toledo. Arcos de Palacio. Tel. 925/22 22 41. Monday–Saturday, 10:30am–1pm and 3:30pm–6pm; Sunday and holidays, 10:30am–1:30pm and 4pm–6pm. 500 ptas.

Museo de Santa Cruz. C/ Miguel de Cervantes, 3. Tel. 925/22 10 36. Monday, 10am–2pm and 4pm–6:30pm; Tuesday–Saturday, 10am–6:30pm; Sunday, 10am–2pm. 200 ptas.

Iglesia de Santo Tomé: El Greco's The Burial of Count Orgaz. Plaza del Conde, 2. Tel. 925/21 02 90. Daily, 10am–1:45pm and 3:30pm–5:45pm (summer hours, open until 6:45pm). 150 pta.

Monasterio de San Juan de los Reyes. C/ de los Reyes Católicos, 17. Tel. 925/22 38 02. Daily, 10am–1:45pm and 3:30pm–5:45pm (summer hours, open until 6:45pm). 150 ptas.

Sinagoga del Tránsito. C/ de Samuel Levi, s/n. Tel. 925/22 36 65. Tuesday–Saturday, 10am–2pm and 4pm–6pm, Sunday 10am–2pm.400 pta. (Free Saturday afternoons and Sunday)

Casa-Museo de El Greco. C/ Samuel Levi, 3. Tel. 925/22 40 46. Tuesday–Saturday, 10am–2pm and 4pm–6pm, Sunday 10am–2pm.400 pta. (free Saturday afternoons and Sunday; free for Seniors.)

Segovia
Catedral de Segovia. Plaza Mayor. Tel. 921/46 22 05. Daily, 9am–7pm (summer), 9:30am–6pm (winter). 250 ptas for entry to cloisters and museum. (Admission free to cathedral)

El Alcázar. Plaza de la Reina. Tel. 921/46 22 05. Daily, 10am–7pm (summer), 10am–6pm (winter). 400 pta.

WHAT TO DO

SHOPPING

As the capital, Madrid draws both people and goods from all over the country. Along with Barcelona, it is Spain's top shopping center. (Though for items positioned almost exclusively to visitors, it's hard to beat Toledo; shopping in the former capital is covered below, separate from Madrid.)

Madrid's best upscale boutiques are located in **Salamanca**, while just about everything else can be found along **Gran Vía** (now less glamorous than it once was), or the streets around the **Puerta del Sol**, especially the pedestrian streets Preciados and del Carmen. The major department stores are found in these three areas as well. Around the **Plaza Mayor** are many souvenir shops and stores selling accessible silver and jewelry. Antiques shopping is focused in the **Latina** area that hosts the weekly Rastro flea market, a true Madrid experience.

Good items to look for in Madrid include antiques, books, classic Spanish fans and embroidered shalls; foodstuffs like cured ham, either jamón de Jabugo or jamón serrano, and chorizo sausage; leather goods, including shoes and handbags; handpainted tiles called *azulejos* and ceramics; and jewelry.

Shopping Hours

Spanish shopping hours for the most part continue to respect the midday lunch closing (only malls and department stores are guaranteed to stay open throughout the day). Open hours are generally Monday–Friday, 9 or 10am–1:30pm or 2pm and 4pm or 5pm–8pm. On Saturdays, stores tend to open from 9:30am–1:30pm. Sunday opening hours remain controversial in this Catholic country, though there has been some movement toward relaxation in recent years.

Individual neighborhoods have their own markets, but two of the biggest for visitors are the Plaza Mayor every Sunday, for stamps and coins, and the famous Rastro flea market around calle Toledo in the La Latina neighborhood. Major department stores include El Corte Inglés, Spain's longtime chain that has several branches in Madrid (c/ Preciados, 1; Goya, 76) and FNAC (c/ Preciados, 28), a French chain that's only slightly less comprehensive in its offerings.

Book lovers have ample opportunity to add to their collections in Madrid. There's an outdoor stand of used and antique books open daily on the tiny Pasadizo de San Ginés sidestreet just off calle Arenal, and on Cuesta de Moyano, near Atocha train station, on weekends. Beginning in late May, a large-scale book fair (**Feria del Libro de Madrid**) takes over Retiro Park, with stalls of diverse publishers set up for several weeks. **Crisol**, a bookstore chain with numerous outlets across the city, has a decent selection of books in English. You'll find stores at Paseo de la Castellana, 90 and Goya, 18. **VIPS**, an all-purpose convenience store, sells art and architecture books, often heavily discounted, in both Spanish and English (Gran Vía, 43 and Serrano, 41).

For **antiques**, head to **El Rastro** (see box, page 48), the flea market for odds-n-ends, on Sundays; it attracts swarms of collectors. In nearby streets are more solid establishments dealing in old *objets d'art*. **Centro de Arte y Antiguedades** (Serrano, 5) has multiple dealers under a single roof, in an attractive old

---

Sale Time

In Spain, sales are held twice annually, beginning the second week of January and the last week of July. Signs announcing *rebajas* are plastered in store windows. Prices continue to drop as stores reduce their leftover inventory in stages, from first, second, and then final *rebajas*, just as the new season's collections filter in.

building, some with very fine and very unusual items.

There are **crafts** of all kinds for sale throughout Madrid, offering a wide variety in originality and skill. Look for glassware, much of it from Mallorca; Valencian porcelain; ceramics from several Spanish regions; woodcarving; embroidered handkerchiefs, napkins, table-cloths, and sheets; collapsible fans like those fluttered by *señoritas* over the centuries; and needlework, such as traditional lace *mantillas* for special occasions and hand-sewn lingerie. The gov-

Madrid shops offer unique items one may be hard-pressed to find elsewhere.

ernment-run store **Artespaña** (Hermosilla 14), has a large selection of crafts, especially items for the home, and **El Arco de los Cuchilleros Artesanía de Hoy** in the Plaza Mayor (at no. 9), has the best selection of crafts from all over Spain, including Spanish fans, embroidered shawls, jewelry, hand-blown glass and ceramics. **Antigua Casa Talavera** (Isabel la Católica, 2) maintains a large selection of hand-painted ceramics, including attractive models from Valencia and Talavera, and tiles.

Spanish **fashion** design has really exploded in the past few years, and much of it is reasonably affordable compared to prices in the rest of Europe and North America. Look for the shops of **Aldolfo Domínguez** (Serrano, 96) and **Ermenegildo Zegna** (Serrano, 21). For fashionable but affordable casual clothes for both sexes, visit **Zara** (Hermosilla, 16; Gran Vía, 32; Princesa, 45).

Higher quality **leather goods** are available in small shops and open-air markets throughout Madrid, including coats, hats, gloves, wallets, and handbags. For chic leather designs, try **Loewe** (Gran Vía, 8 and Serrano, 26), Spain's top luxury clothier. It has great, although expensive luggage and handbags.

There's a wide variety of **gift items** available. Lladró porcelain figures are a good buy. **Lladró Tienda Madrid** (Serrano, 68) and **Artestilo Lladró** (Paseo del Prado, 10) have a wide selection. **Casa Yusta** (Plaza Mayor, 30) is a legendary hatmaker; it also sells souvenir items (such as swords and shields). Stylish fans and shawls can be found at **Casa de Diego** (Puerta del Sol, 12) and **Almoraima** (Plaza Mayor, 12). **Perlas Majorica** (Gran Vía, 39) has terrific, but not inexpensive, faux pearls from Majorca.

Spanish music on compact disc or tape makes a good souvenir. Look for flamenco — try Camarón de la Isla, Paco de Lucía, Tomatito, Pata Negra, or Miguel Poveda — or *rock en español* (Spanish rock). Good selections are found at **Virgin Megastore** (Serrano, 61), **FNAC** (Preciados 28) or **Madrid Rock** (Gran Vía), the latter with excellent sales bins in back.

Spanish **shoes** are stylish and can be very affordable during sales. Both **Yanko** (Gran Vía, 40) and **Calzados Bravo** (Gran Vía, 31 and 68; Princesa, 58; Goya, 43) have good selections of shoes for both sexes.

Majorca (Velázquez, 59) is a gourmet shop with a good selection of **Spanish wines**, including sherry (jerez), and Rioja and Ribera del Duero red and white *crianzas, reservas* and *gran reservas.*

Shopping in Toledo

With so many tourists darting in and out of Toledo, one of the top crafts centers in Spain, it's no surprise that vendors are ready for them. The tiny streets are lined with souvenir shops selling cheap trinkets and expensive, one-of-a-kind items. The city's Moorish roots are present in the distinctive black-and-gold **damascene** — an ancient Moorish practice of inlaying gold (and sometimes copper or silver) against a background of matte black steel. You'll find rings, letter-openers, and many other damascene souvenirs. Look for better, handcrafted items. **Swords**, a throwback to the Middle Ages, are also hugely popular (though potentially difficult to carry back on airplanes). Good spots for both items are **Braojos** (Arco de Palacio, 5 and Comercio, 44), **Casa Bermejo** (c/ Airosas, 5), and **Felipe Suárez** (Paseo de los Canónigos).

You can use your new sword to cut through some Toledo **marzipan** (*marzapan* in Spanish). Look for the sweet stuff at **Pastelerías Santo Tomé** (c/ Santo Tomé, 5 and Plaza Zocodover, 7), **Casa Telesforo** (Plaza de Zocodover, 13), and **Pastelería Casado** (Cuesta del Alcázar, 11).

Every Tuesday, Toledo's Paseo del Carmen is the site of a large outdoor **market.** Here you can spy on the shouting, shoving, and color of provincial Spain. The street market caters to practical local needs—basic clothing and household goods.

Embroidery from provincial towns outside Toledo is sold in many shops, alongside local **pottery** and traditional ceram-

Tax Back

Non-EU residents can reclaim IVA tax (Value Added Tax, anything from 6 to 33 percent depending on the type of goods); if purchases are substantial (you must spend at least 15,000 ptas. in a single store), it is certainly worthwhile to fill out the forms in the shop. The refund can be credited to your credit card at the airport or mailed to your home address after your return. You must show your purchases to the customs inspector on departure and give him the appropriate forms (which you get from stores advertising "Tax Refund")

ics from **Talavera de la Reina**, a small town renowned for the blue-and-yellow **ceramics** it has produced since the 15th century. The town (76 km/47 miles west of Madrid) is replete with ceramics vendors, as are the roads leading to town. To get to Talavera, take C-503 west from Toledo. The local women of the small towns **Orpesa** (24 km/15 miles from Talavera) and **Lagartera** (7 km/4 mi. beyond Orpesa) produce richly embroidered tablecloths and other linens.

ENTERTAINMENT

Bullfighting

The *corrida,* the bullfight, is an enduring symbol of macho, death-obsessed Spain. It is a spectacle of flamboyance and fate, violence and grace. And Madrid is indisputably the world's bullfighting capital. No matter how much of a sensation a bullfighter may have achieved in the provinces, he hasn't hit the big time until he wins the cheers of *Madrileños.*

You may not like what you see, you may swear never to return to it, or you may become an outright *aficionado.* Whatever your reaction, you'll have to admit there's nothing like it in the world: man against bull, skill against instinct. For the bull, the outcome is certain; for the matador, less so. At the outset of the fight, the matador meets the bull, takes his measure, and be-

Buying a ticket to a bullfight labeled "sol," "sombra," or "sol y sombra" is no mere distinction of what side of the stadium your seat is on. It determines whether you'll be baking in the sizzling Spanish sun (sol), relaxing in the shade (sombra), or having a bit of both (sol y sombra) as the afternoon wears on. Sombra seats cost more, but are well worth the extra pesetas (which you would end up spending on sunscreen anyway); more activity takes place in the shaded part of the stadium, as well. Bullfighting season lasts from May to October.

gins to tire him using the big red and yellow *capote.*

After these preliminaries, the first *tercio* (third) begins when the *picador,* a mounted spearman in Sancho Panza costume, lances the bull's shoulder muscles. Then, in the second *tercio,* the deft *banderilleros* stab long darts into the animal's shoulders. In the third *tercio,* the matador returns to run the bull through a long series of passes, using the dark-red *muleta* cape, eventually dom-

The high art of bullfighting reveals the grace and skill within every true Spaniard.

inating the beast. Finally, as the bull awaits its death, the *torero* lunges for the kill.

The spectacle is certainly not for everyone—not even for every Spaniard, but it is something that remains very much a part of Spanish life.

Madrid's bullring, **Plaza de Toros de Las Ventas** (c/ de Alcalá, 237; Metro: Ventas), seats 23,000 spectators, but buying a ticket is not always easy. Your hotel desk clerk can usually help—but at a significant mark-up for the ticket agent and a tip for the clerk. Travel agencies run tours for the afternoon, which include transport, tickets, and a commentary. However you go, and whether you sit in the *sol* (sun) or *sombra* (shade), invest a few pesetas in comfort: rent a cushion so you don't spend the afternoon sitting on bare concrete.

Normally, Sunday afternoons are reserved for bullfights. But during the San Isidro fiestas in May, Madrid has bullfights every day for more than two weeks. Tickets are extremely dif-

A fiesta in the windmill country of La Mancha brings out the finery of local folk dancers.

ficult to secure. For tickets, contact **Localidades García,** Plaza del Carmen, 1 (Tel. 91/531 27 32) or **TEYCI,** calle Goya, 7 (Tel. 91/576 45 32).

Flamenco

Spain's best-known art form, after the bullfight, is flamenco—a feast of percussive guitars, staccato heels, and songs that gush from the soul. Many of the songs resemble the wailing of Arab music—which may be a clue to the flamenco's origins, though not all "flamencologists" agree.

Madrid's flamenco nightclubs attract huge crowds, including tourists who don't usually go to nightclubs or stay up after midnight. The anguished chants and compelling rhythms generate an electricity that defies cultural barriers.

There are two main groups of songs: one, bouncier and more cheerful, is known as the *cante chico* (a light tune). The second group of songs, called *cante jondo,* deals with love and death (all the human drama), done in the slow, piercing style of the great flamenco singers. Purists say the talent in a *tablao flamenco* in Madrid is rarely up to top Andalusian standards.

This may or may not be true, depending on the artists — though the quality of dancing is generally excellent — but it is for most a memorable and uniquely Spanish night out, an overwhelming experience for the eyes and ears.

Clubs: **Café de Chinitas** (calle Torija, 7; Tel. 91/547 15 02; Metro: Santo Domingo) is the best-known, most touristed, and most expensive of the Madrid clubs. **Corral de la Morería** (Morería, 7; Tel. 91/565 81 46; Metro: La Latina) is very lively. **Casa Patas** (Cañizares, 10; Tel. 91/369 04 96; Metro: Antón Martín) is a restaurant-bar with flamenco shows in a back room (Mon-Thur at 10:30pm, Fri and Sat at midnight). Shows are cheaper, more intimate and perhaps the most authentic in Madrid. **La Soleá** near Plaza San Andrés (c/ Cava Baja, 27) has participatory (and occasionally incendiary) flamenco and *sevillanas* performances in one of Madrid's top tapas areas.

Late-Night Madrid

Europe's most indefatigable night people, Madrileños choose from a profusion of bars and clubs. There are bohemian cafés, dark *boîtes* staffed with professional drinking partners, deafening discothèques, English-style and Irish pubs and beer halls, and live jazz and folk-music clubs. In the summertime the open-air bars and streetside cafés provide a more peaceful and relaxing atmosphere.

Travel agencies run Madrid-by-night tours, taking in a couple of the top floorshows. Normally the all-inclusive price covers dinner and a quota of drinks.

Bars & Cafés. Two areas crammed with bars and cafes are: **calle de las Huertas,** between the Plaza Mayor and Paseo del Prado, and the area around **Plaza Dos de Mayo,** in the Malasaña district just north of the center. A favorite of beer drinkers is **Cervecería Alemana** (Plaza de Santa Ana, 6), a beer hall with a young, cheerful crowd. Plaza de Santa Ana itself is very lively, full of barhoppers most nights of the week. **Los Gabrieles** (Echegaray, 17) has wall-to-wall color tiles inside, a great spot at any time but very popular late at night. **Antigua Casa Angel Sierra**, on the Plaza de Chueca, in the funky Chueca neighborhood, is one of Madrid's most atmospheric taverns, with hand-pulled vermouth and lots of local barrio cheer. Sleekly art deco **Chicote** (Gran Vía, 12) is a classic Madrid cocktail bar, where Orson Wells, Ava Gardner, Frank Sinatra, Ernest Hemingway and other famous faces imbibed.

Cafes & terrazas. Plaza Mayor and Plaza Santa Ana have several cafes that get going in early evening before more serious and louder drinkers arrive. Summer brings *terrazas* (open-air bars) along the Paseo de la Castellana. An institution in Madrid for literary types is the late-19th century Café Gijón (Paseo de Recoletos, 21), while on Plaza de Oriente, near the Royal Palace is Café de Oriente (Plaza de Oriente, 2), sitting on the foundation of a 17th-century convent. Another classic old world spot is Comercial (Ctra. de Bilbao, 7).

Live music clubs. There are plenty of places in Madrid for live jazz and Latin music. **Café Central** (Plaza del Ángel, 10; Tel 91/369 41 43) is a sophisticated jazz cafe near Plaza de Santa Ana with nightly music. **Populart** (calle de las

---

Hunger Pains

Madrileños stave off bed even longer by hitting the *chocolatería* or *churrería* — a place to get *chocolate con churros* — in the wee hours. *Churros* are thick fingers of deep-fried dough, usually served with rich hot chocolate for dunking. At 5 or 6am, a line may already be forming. You won't believe how crowded these places can get at 6am. Madrid's classic *churros* place is **Churrería de San Ginés**, on Pasadizo de San Ginés, between calle Mayor and Arenal in the heart of Viejo Madrid.

Huertas, 22; Tel. 91/429 84 07) has a more wide-ranging lineup, including jazz, reggae and blues.

Discos. Discos are usually open until almost breakfast, and since staying out late is the point in Madrid, they continue to be very popular, especially with late-teen and early-20s crowds. Most don't really throb until about 2am or 3am. One of the city's longest-running discos is **Pacha** (c/ Barceló, 11.). Closed for awhile, it has re-opened without losing a beat. **Joy Eslava** (c/ de Arenal, 11) is a longtime hipster disco that still attracts its share of beautiful people and entertainers. **Palacio Gaviria** (c/ de Arenal, 9) is a wild place with "13 Elizabethan lounges" in a 19th-century palace, and offerings ranging from high-throttle disco to ballroom dancing.

Concerts & Opera. Two resident symphony orchestras — the National Orchestra and the Spanish Radio and Television Symphony Orchestra — maintain a regular schedule of concerts for serious music fans in Madrid. Regular seasons of ballet and opera are also held. Madrid's performing arts companies — including the Ballet Nacional de España, Orquesta Sinfónica de Madrid and Orquesta Nacional de España — are among the best in Spain. Look also for the world-famous flamenco troupe of Antonio Canales, Ballet Flamenco Antonio Canales.

Revelers in Toledo enjoy a celebration in the Cathedral Square.

Madrid's opera house, the **Teatro Real,** one of the most advanced opera houses in Europe, features big-name productions (box office: Plaza Isabel II, s/n; Tel. 91/516 06 06 or 91/516 06 60). Guided tours are available Tues-Fri, Sat and Sun. The **Auditorio Nacional de Música** (Príncipe de Vergara, 146; Tel. 91/337 01 00) has opera from January–July and excellent classical music concerts from October–June. **Teatro Calderón** (calle Atocha, 18; Tel. 91/632 01 14) programs well-known operas with tourist appeal, such as Rossini's *The Barber of Seville.*

Zarzuela. This uniquely Spanish form of operetta is much appreciated in Madrid, though its popularity has declined since the 1890s. The *zarzuela* comes in both lighthearted and serious varieties and is entertaining even if you don't understand the language. The **Teatro Lírico Nacional de la Zarzuela**, (Jovellanos, 4; Tel. 91/524 54 00) and Centro Cultural de la Villa (Plaza de Colón; Tel. 91/575 60 80) both have performances.

Theater. Spain's dramatic tradition is long and glorious. In dozens of Madrid theatres, classical and contemporary foreign and Spanish works are performed, usually twice a night. Ability to understand Spanish—or ability not to care that you don't—is a must. The Teatro Albéniz (calle Paz, 11; Tel. 91/531 83 11) features theater as well as dance and occasional zarzuela. Teatro Nuevo Apolo (Plaza de Tirso de Molina, 1; Tel. 91/429 52 38) often has popular international musicals. Teatro de la Comedia (calle Príncipe, 14; Tel. 91/521 49 31), despite the name, doesn't put on only comedies, but classic Spanish works, by playwrights like García Lorca and Lope de Vega. Teatro Español (Príncipe, 25; Tel. 91/429 03 18) programs a wide variety of Spanish plays.

Fiestas. A fiesta in any Spanish city or village, however insignificant, will reveal a spirit and pageantry to be found nowhere else. Check local publications, ask at the tourist office or your hotel to be sure you don't miss some regional festival. The big ones in Madrid are **San Isidro**, held during two weeks in the middle of May, and the *castizo fiestas* de San Lorenzo, San Cayetano and La Virgen de la Paloma, all held during the second week of August in the working-class neighborhoods of La Latina and Lavapiés.

SPORTS

Spectator Sports

Fútbol (football/soccer). The world's number one sport is top dog in Spain. **Real Madrid** plays at Estadio Santiago Bernabéu (c/ Concha Esquina, s/n). **Atlético Madrid** calls home Estadio Vicente Calderón (Paseo de la Virgen del Puerto, 67), in southwest Madrid. The season lasts from September to May.
Horse racing. Afternoons at the Hipódromo de la Zarzuela on the La Coruña road, 7 km/4 miles from central Madrid.
Pelota. The lightning fast Basque ball game, known in some circles as *jai alai,* can be witnessed afternoons at Frontón Madrid, (c/ del Doctor Cortezo, 10).
Auto racing. Championship trials at the Jarama circuit, on the road to Burgos, 26 km/16 miles north of Madrid.

Participant Sports

Golf. Half a dozen golf courses in the Madrid area operate year-round. Greens are open to non-members on payment of a substantial greens fee. Contact the **Real Federación Española de Golf.** Capitán Haya 9, 28020 Madrid, or a Spanish Tourism Office (see 123) abroad for a detailed pamphlet, "Golf in Spain."
Skiing. From December to April, the Guadarrama mountains north of Madrid become a major ski area. The scenery and facilities are first-rate, and all equipment may be hired. The most highly developed resort is Navacerrada, only 60 km/37 miles

Calendar of Events

As you plan your excursions, it is worth checking additional details of festivals and fairs around the country with tourist information offices.

January *Día de los Reyes* (Three Kings Calvacade). Procession through streets commemorating kings' pilgrimage to meet baby Jesus. Takes place in the first week of the month.

February *Carnaval.* Week before Lent celebrated with the curious *Entierro de la Sardina* (Burial of the Sardine) on Paseo de la Florida. *Zamarramala, Segovia Province.* Santa Agueda festivals, medieval costumes, and even older customs.

ARCO (Contemporary Art Fair). Spain's largest international art fair, usually the second week in February.

March/April *Semana Santa (Holy Week).* Every town and city has striking processions of the penitent and other religious manifestations. In cities with famous cathedrals, such as Toledo and Segovia, the spectacle is unforgettable. The colorful town of Cuenca, 165 km (100 miles) southeast of Madrid, is noted for its splendid processions.

May *Madrid: Fiestas de San Isidro* (St. Isidore the Husbandman), the capital's patron saint. Half a month of neighborhood parties, contests, plays, concerts, and daily bullfights.

June *Toledo: Corpus Christi.* The Spanish primate leads a solemn religious procession through the medieval streets.

Toledo Province: Camuñas. An ancient religious play is presented in mime, with spectacular costumes.

Fiestas de San Juan and San Pedro. Dances, bullfights, fireworks. June 17-24.

July *Ávila.* Summer festival with poetry, art, theatre, sports, bullfights, and fun, all outdoors.

August *Madrid: Castizo fiestas* of San Caeyetano, San Lorenzo and La Virgen de la Paloma. August 15th is a major national holiday and many towns have local celebrations on this day.

September *Ávila Province: Candeleda.* Pilgrimage of Our Lady of Chilla, medieval religious ceremonies plus dancing and bullfights.

October *Toledo Province: Consuegra.* Saffron Rose Festival in the heart of windmill country of La Mancha.

December *Nochevieja* (New Year's Eve). Traditional celebration in Madrid's Puerta del Sol, swallowing grapes at each chime of the clock.

Madrid played host to the 1982 World Cup, a major event indeed for this soccer-loving country.

from Madrid by car or bus. The only snag is that the slopes are packed with *Madrileños* every weekend and on holidays.

Several other areas within easy range of the capital may be less congested. For further information, consult the **Federación Española Deportes de Invierno**, (Spanish Winter Sports Federation), Infanta María Teresa 14, 28016 Madrid.

Elsewhere in Madrid, various sports facilities cater to many interests. You'll find **tennis** courts, **polo** grounds, **squash** courts, **swimming** pools, and **riding** stables.

MADRID FOR CHILDREN

Casa de Campo. This wide expanse of 4,000 acres, once royal hunting grounds, north of Plaza de España has a lake (with rowboats), theme park (Parque de Atracciones), swimming pool, sailing lake, and ultra-modern zoo (Parque Zoológico). For added excitement, children love to take the cable car that soars above the city (*teleférico* station in Paseo del Pintor Rosales).

Retiro Park. Near the Prado Museum, this exciting venue has acrobats, clowns, and all sorts of other sideshows during summer, as well as paddleboats on the small lake.

EATING OUT

Madrid is one of the great dining capitals in Spain: the restaurants in this melting pot represent all regional specialties plus a constantly widening array of international choices. In addition to fine dining, one of the most appetizing culinary options in Madrid is the *tapeo*—the tapas crawl—which has been raised to an art form.

Regional cuisine varies greatly, but Spanish cooking is never overly spicy; in fact, a few Castilian dishes may seem underseasoned. Pepper is rarely served at the table; you'll need to ask for *pimienta negra*.

Mealtimes

For many visitors, dining hours in Spain take some getting used to. Madrileños eat lunch and dinner especially late by most standards. Lunch is served between 1pm and 4pm, but usually isn't eaten until 2:30 or 3pm. Dinner is served between 8:30 or 9pm and 11:30, though most locals are likely to aim for 10pm and on weekends they often don't sit down to dinner until 11:30pm or after midnight. Visitors aren't required to dine as late as locals, of course — though if you enter the restaurant soon after the doors have swung open, you are likely to find yourself dining alone. Adopt the Spanish system — pace yourself for the late hours by sampling tapas at your normal dinner time.

Restaurants and Menus

When eating out, Spaniards generally eat three courses at both lunch and dinner, including dessert and coffee. However, it's not uncommon to share a first course, or to order *un sólo plato*—just a main course—if you're not that hungry or looking to economize. Many restaurants offer a lunchtime *menú del día* or *menú de la casa*, a daily set menu that's one of the best dining bargains in Europe. For a fixed price (often US $10-15), you'll get: appetizer, often soup or salad; main dish; and dessert (ice-cream, a piece of fruit or pastry), plus wine, beer, or bottled water, and bread. Typically, the cost is about half of what you'd expect to pay if you ordered from the regular menu. Most Spaniards will also order the *menú,* so

> If you request the "menu," the waiter will probably think the fixed-price meal is what you mean (*menú del día, menú de la casa*). If you want to look at the full list of dishes available, ask for *la carta.*

there's no need to think you're ordering the "tourist special."

Reservations are recommended at Madrid's nicer restaurants. Your menu and restaurant bill automatically include taxes and service charges, but it's customary to leave a tip of between five and 10 percent.

Formal sit-down meals are available in restaurants and *cafeterías.* The first offers a full menu, often with a pre-fixe menu available; the latter usually focuses on *platos combinados,* or a combined plate with a main course and accompaniment like fries or salad served on the same plate. Restaurants feature a grading system, from five forks to one, marked on the door of the restaurant, which is supposed to announce the category, though the signs are not always prominently displayed. The system is an indication of price and grades the facilities and service, not the quality of the food.

Most cafés and bars (called *tabernas, bodegas,* and even *cervecerías*) serve food, often of a very high standard. There you can have a selection of *tapas,* sandwiches (*bocadillos*), or limited *platos combinados. Tascas* (variably referred to as *mesones* and *tabernas*) are informal haunts which serve snacks with wine or beer. *Cafés* serve coffee, drinks, and snacks, and are almost always open. At many bars and tascas, prices are higher if you sit at a table rather than at the bar. Cafés with outdoor seating often charge more to sit outside.

The most insignificant meal of the day in Spain is breakfast — except at hotels, which proffer mega-buffets as money-makers or enticements. (Check to see if breakfast is included in the room price at your hotel; if not, the hefty price may prompt you to check out the nearest café or cafeteria.) As for breakfast pastries, try *churros*, fritters often made before your eyes. You absolutely must dunk *churros* in your coffee, or try them as the Spaniards do with very thick and rich hot chocolate. The occasional cafeteria may serve not only great coffee but an "English breakfast" of bacon and eggs, too.

> *Tapa* means "lid," a nickname derived from the little plate which covered the beverage glass and carried the snack, back in the day when a drink automatically came with a free morsel.

Tasty Tapas

Tapas — the often not-so-small snacks that Spanish bars and cafés are world-famous for — come in dozens of delicious preparations, from appetizers such as olives and salted almonds to vegetable salads, fried squid, chilled shrimp, lobster mayonnaise, sausage slices, meatballs, spiced potatoes, and goat cheese. The list is virtually endless, and can be surprisingly creative, especially at Basque tapas joints. A small plate is called a *porción*. A larger serving, meant to be shared, is a *ración*, and half of this, a *media-ración*. Tapas are usually available throughout the day.

Some bars specialize in *tapas*, often featuring a long row of dishes, hot and cold, for you to pick from. Often bars will list their tapas on a blackboard on the sidewalk; a menu of 50 items is not uncommon. Portions are larger now that you're paying for them: perhaps five different choices is enough to substitute for a conventional main course. You don't need to know the tapa names — just point. Be on the lookout for *boquerones*, white anchovies freshly prepared in

---

El Tapeo: Touring the Tascas

Madrid is rife with atmospheric tascas—bars where tapas grazing (*el tapeo*), a daily pursuit for most Madrileños, is the main order of the day. The best areas are the La Latina and Huertas districts of Old Madrid; the following is merely a selection, as there are hundreds of tascas to choose from across Madrid. More than two centuries old, with bulls's heads and other taurine memorabilia on the walls, **Taberna de Antonio Sánchez** is legendary (Mesón de Paredes, 13). On one of Madrid's most trafficked tapas streets, **Taberna Almendo 13** (c/ Almendro, 13) is a great corner place specializing in *fino* and *manzanilla* (dry sherry) and serving a wide variety of tapas and *raciones* to a noisy local crowd. **La Taberna Angosta,** on a winding old Moorish street just west of Plaza San Andrés (c/ Mancebosl, 6) has excellent homemade pâtés and good wine. **Taberna de Cien Vinos** (del Nuncio, 17) means the tavern of 100 wines, but it has many more than that. It also has some great tapas, including roast beef and salt cod. **Casa Antonio** (Latoneros, 10) is a Madrid classic, with a zinc bar, Moorish tiles and bright red doors. The doors fling open and people spill out into the street. **Casa del Labra** (c/ Tetuán, 12) is a great old spot near the Puerta del Sol serving homemade *croquetas* and *bacalao* (cod fried in batter). **Lhardy** (San Jerónimo, 8) is one of the city's fanciest restaurants, but the landmark 1839 building also has a gorgeously conserved little pastry shop/café serving more affordable stand-up canapés. The 18th-century cave-like bars built right into the wall outside the Plaza Mayor (on Cava San Miguel) are more touristy. Many have live music and alcohol-fueled sing-alongs.

vinegar, oil, and garlic; and, most common of all on tapa counters, the classic *tortilla española*, an omelette with potatoes and onions, fried in olive oil until golden.

Castilian Specialities

Cocido madrileño is unique to Madrid, though it superficially resembles the hotpot or stew found in other regions of Spain. The meal often starts with *sopa de cocido* (the broth resulting from boiling the ingredients for the next course), before moving to the *cocido* itself: beef, ham, sausage, chickpeas, cabbage, turnip, onion, garlic, potatoes.

Sopa castellana (sopa de ajo). Baked garlic soup, not nearly as strong as it sounds. At the last moment, a raw egg is added; by the time it reaches the table, the egg is well poached.

Callos a la madrileña. By any other name, stewed tripe. But the spicy dark sauce makes all the difference. It's a great local favorite if you've the stomach for it.

Besugo al horno. Sea-bream poached in a wine sauce.

Cochinillo asado. Tender Castilian suckling pig roasted to a golden crispness.

Cordero asado. Roast lamb, often a gargantuan helping.

Jamón serrano (jamón de Jabugo): One of spaniards' favorite tapas, thinly sliced cured ham. Rarely cheap, but always exquisite.

This taberna outside Plaza Major is a welcome sight for any weary traveler.

Regional Specialties

Andalucía: *gazpacho* (pronounced gath-patcho) is the famous "liquid salad," so refreshing on a summer day. A chilled, highly flavored soup to which chopped tomatoes, peppers, cucumbers, onions, and croutons are added to taste.

Valencia: One of Spain's great dishes, *paella* (pronounced pie-ay-ya) is named after the black iron pan in which saffron rice is cooked, with such ingredients as: squid, sausage, shrimp, rabbit, chicken, mussels, onion, peppers, peas, beans, tomatoes, garlic. Authentic *paella* is served at lunchtime, cooked to order.

Asturias: *fabada,* a variation on Madrid's famouse *cocido,* but based largely upon white beans and sausage.

Navarra: *trucha a la navarra,* grilled trout with a stuffed with a slice of ham.

Galicia: *caldo gallego,* a rich vegetable soup.

Basque country: A wide variety of rich fish dishes come from Spain's top gourmet region in the north. Try *bacalao al pil pil* (cod in hot garlic sauce), *merluza a la vasca* (hake in a casserole with a thick sauce), or *angulas a la bilbaína* (eels in a hot olive-oil and garlic sauce, eaten with a wooden fork).

Drinks

In Madrid you'll find fine wines from across Spain, including the regions of La Rioja, Navarra, Ribiera del Duero, and Penedés. Also try *cava,* Catalonia's sparkling wine.

If you just say *tinto* (red) or *blanco* (white) when asked for your choice of *vino,* you'll get the house wine. You may get a bottle or a carafe. Many diners add a bit of bubbly mineral water into their house wine to smooth out a heavy or harsh flavor.

Spanish beers, in bottles or on draft (*caña*), are generally light and refreshing. *Sangría* is a favorite summer wine and fruit mixture — every bar has its own recipe. To many, Spain means sherry (*jerez*) from the south (near Jerez de la Frontera).

The Plaza Segovia Nueva, in the heart of la Latina, is home to tapas eateries.

The pale, dry *fino* is sometimes drunk not only as an apéritif but with soup and fish courses. Rich, dark *oloroso* goes well after dinner. Spanish brandy varies: you usually get what you pay for. Other spirits are made under license in Spain, and are usually much cheaper than imported Scotch whisky, for example.

Coffee is can be served black (*café solo*), with a spot of milk (*café cortado*), or half hot milk (*café con leche*).

To Help You Order…

Could we have a table?	**¿Nos puede dar una mesa, por favor?**
Do you have a set menu?	**¿Tiene un menú del día?**
I'd like a/an/some…	**Quisiera…**
Menu	**la carta**
The check, please	**La cuenta, por favor**

The Basics…

beer	**cerveza**	bread	**pan**
mineral water	**agua mineral**	napkin	**servilleta**
cutlery	**los cubiertos**	potatoes	**patatas**
dessert	**postre**	rice	**arroz**
fish	**pescado**	salad	**ensalada**
fruit	**fruta**	sandwich	**bocadillo**
glass	**vaso**	sugar	**azúcar**
ice cream	**helado**	tea	**té**

| meat | **carne** | (iced) water | **agua (fresca)** |
| menu | **la carta** | wine | **vino** |

...and Read the Menu

langosta	**spiny lobster**	anchoas	**anchovies**
albóndigas	**meat balls**	almejas	**baby clams**
atún	**tuna**	mariscos	**shellfish**
calamares	**squid**	ostras	**oysters**
pastel	**cake**	cangrejo	**crab**
pimiento	**green pepper**	caracoles	**snails**
pollo	**chicken**	cerdo	**pork**
pulpitos	**baby octopus**	chuleta	**pork chops**
salsa	**sauce**	ternera	**veal**
entremeses	**hors-d'oeuvre**	trucha	**trout**
gambas	**prawns**	uvas	**grapes**
verduras	**vegetables**	judías	**beans**

Tapas

Aceitunas	olives
Chorizo	cured sausage
Croquetas	croquettes (fish or chicken)
Morcilla	blood sausage
Queso	cheese
Champiñones	mushrooms fried in garlic
Tortilla española	potato omelette

Preparations

al ajillo	in garlic
a la parilla/a la plancha	grilled
asado	roasted
poco hecho/al punto/	rare/medium-rare/
muy hecho	well done
salteado	sautéed

HANDY TRAVEL TIPS

An A–Z Summary of Practical Information

A

ACCOMMODATIONS *(hotel; alojamiento)* (See also the list of RECOMMENDED HOTELS starting on page 126)
Spanish hotels are rated by a star system, with five-star deluxe the top grade. The classifications often seem arbitrary; some two- and three-star places will have the same quality as a hotel with a higher rating. About two-thirds of the city's hotels fall into the three- and four-star categories. Breakfast is rarely included in the room rate, and hotels are subject to a seven percent IVA (value added) tax.

Hotel-reservation desks are found at Barajas Airport, at Chamartín and Atocha railway stations, and in the Torre de Madrid on Plaza de España. Before taking a room, the guest fills out a form with hotel category, room number, and price, and signs it.

I'd like a double/single room.	**Quisiera una habitación doble/sencilla.**
with/without bath/shower	**con/sin baño/ducha**
double bed	**cama matrimonial**
What's the rate per night?	**¿Cuál es el precio por noche?**
Is breakfast included in the room rate?	**¿Está incluído el desayuno?**
Where's an inexpensive hotel?	**¿Dónde hay un hotel económico?**

AIRPORT *(aeropuerto)*
Barajas International Airport (Tel. 91/393 60 00 or 91/305 83 43), 15 km (9 miles) east of Madrid, handles domestic and international flights. Arriving passengers will find luggage trolleys. Taxis are readily available (the fare should be under 3,000 ptas. to downtown, including extra charges for baggage and airport pickup). Air-conditioned airport buses (385 ptas.) leave every 15 minutes for the city terminal beneath Plaza de Colón. The trip normally takes 30 to 45 minutes. Leave more time for the return trip, as traffic delays could easily add another hour.

Madrid

When making hotel reservations, you may wish ask your hotel about the **Aero City** service — an airport shuttle service that will pick you up at the airport and deliver you to your hotel, or vice-versa, for about 1,000 ptas. less than a taxi. Participating hotels have reservation forms to fill out if you want a lift back to the airport.

Line 8 of the Madrid Metro (subway), a long-awaited project, should be up and running to Barajas airport (it was originally scheduled to open in December 1999 but was delayed). The tourist information booth will be able to direct you to it and the stop closest to your hotel.

Taxi!	**¡Taxi!**
Where's the bus for downtown?	**¿Dónde está el autobús para el centro?**

B

BUDGETING FOR YOUR TRIP

With a favorable exchange rate, most items in Madrid are somewhat cheaper than other major European cities, such as London, Paris or Rome.

Transportation to Madrid. For Europeans, Madrid is a short, direct flight away. Regularly scheduled flights may not be inexpensive, but you are likely to find a fair choice of discounts and charter flights. For those traveling from beyond Europe, the flight will be a considerably greater expenditure and portion of your overall budget, though you may also be able to find packages and specials.

Accommodations. Hotels in Madrid are the most expensive in Spain. Still, many at the three- and four-star rating are comparatively good values. Keep in mind that most do not include breakfast or the 7% IVA (value added) tax. See approximate prices in the following section, "Recommended Hotels."

Meals. Restaurant prices are not inexpensive, though with a favorable exchange rate, even top-rated restaurants may be surprisingly affordable compared to most European capitals. The Spanish institution, the *menú del día*, a pre-fixe midday meal, is an excellent bargain, often costing no more than US $10-15 for a 3-course meal. Spanish wines are an excellent deal, even in fine restaurants.

Local transportation. Public transportation within the city — buses and the Metro, or subway — is inexpensive, and taxis are very affordable and a good way to get around. Car rentals, though, can also be much less expensive than in other European countries.

Incidentals. Your major expenses will be excursions, entertainment and daytime sporting activities. Nightclub and disco cover charges are high, as are drinks once inside.

C

CAR RENTAL/HIRE *(coche de alquiler)* See also DRIVING.
A rental car is best if you wish to make several side trips from Madrid in a short amount of time. Otherwise, there's good public transportation to all the destinations discussed in this book, and there's no need to rent a car just to get around in Madrid (in fact, traffic, driving mania, and parking would make the exercise foolhardy).

Major international — Avis, Hertz, Budget, National, Kemwell — and Spanish national rental companies are located in the airport. A value-added tax (IVA) of 15% is added to the total charge, but will have been included if you have pre-paid the car hire before arrival (normally the way to obtain the lowest rates). Third-party insurance is required and included, but full collision coverage is advisable as well. Many credit cards automatically include this if you use the card to pay for the car, but be sure to verify this before departure.

Renters must be 21 and have had a license for at least 6 months. Rental companies will accept your home country's national driver's license. Renting at an airport may incur a surcharge of up to US $10.

Madrid

I'd like to rent a car (tomorrow).	**Quisiera alquilar un coche (para mañana).**
for one day/a week	**por un día/una semana**
Please include full insurance.	**Haga el favor de incluir el seguro a todo riesgo.**
Unleaded gasoline	**petrol sin plomo**
Fill it up	**Lleno, por favor**

CLIMATE

You'd be wise to avoid Madrid in July and August, as many *Madrileños* do. The heat is stifling, and many restaurants and sites of interest close up. In winter months, cold and grayness are often alleviated by bright, mild spells. But it can be very cold at times, too, with sub-zero temperatures, snow, and icy winds from the mountains.

Spring or autumn are the best seasons by far to travel to Madrid and surroundings: you're likely to get perfect temperatures, low humidity and some of the brightest sunshine in Europe.

Average temperatures:

	J	F	M	A	M	J	J	A	S	O	N	D
max. °F	47	52	59	65	70	80	87	85	77	65	55	48
°C	8	11	15	18	21	26	30	29	25	18	13	9
min. °F	35	36	41	45	50	58	63	63	57	49	42	36
°C	2	2	5	7	10	14	17	17	14	9	5	2

Average hours of sunshine per day:

J	F	M	A	M	J	J	A	S	O	N	D
5	6	6	8	9	11	12	11	9	7	5	4

CLOTHING

Madrid's traditional formality of dress has relaxed under the influence of the younger generation. Businessmen often wear an open-collar shirt in summer. Still, resort wear would be inappropriate in this big, sophisticated city and brings stares when worn by the unwary. A few upper-echelon restaurants require jackets and ties for men. On visits to churches, it's best to wear modest clothing rather than tank tops and cut-off shorts—though in the heat of summer, no one is likely to prohibit you from entering in walking shorts.

Do I need a jacket? A tie?	**¿Se necesita una americana? ¿Una corbata?**

CRIME AND SAFETY (see also POLICE AND EMERGENCIES)
Though Madrid should not be considered dangerous enough to deter anyone from visiting, there are pockets where tourists should certainly be on guard. These areas include the Prado Museum (where scams are often perpetrated); Rastro weekend flea market; Puerta del Sol; Plaza Mayor; Plaza de Toros bullring; on the Metro; or any large street gathering. The most common crimes are the snatching of handbags and cameras or picking of pockets.

Don't leave luggage unattended; don't carry more money on your person than you'll need for daily expenses; use the hotel safe deposit for larger sums and valuables; in crowds around street attractions and sports events, be on your guard against pickpockets; reject offers of flowers or other objects from street peddlers — they may be after your purse; wear cameras strapped crosswise on the body; don't leave video cameras, radios, cassettes, and valuables in view inside your car, even when locked; photocopy personal documents and leave the originals in your hotel.

I want to report a theft.	**Quiero denunciar un robo.**
My ticket/wallet/passport has been stolen.	**Me han robado mi billete/ cartera/pasaporte.**

CUSTOMS (*aduana*) **AND ENTRY REQUIREMENTS** (See also EMBASSIES, CONSULATES AND HIGH COMISSIONS on page 103)
All citizens of the US, the UK, Canada, Australia and New Zealand (adults and children) need is a valid passport to enter Spain (and stay for up to 90 days). For members of the streamlined European Union,

the process is harmless: they won't even get their passport stamped (though they still need to carry it). Citizens of South Africa need a visa in order to visit Spain. Full information on passport and visa regulations is available from the Spanish Embassy in your country.

As Spain is part of the European Union (EU), free exchange of non-duty-free items for personal use is permitted between Spain and UE countries. However, duty-free items are still subject to restrictions. There are no limits on the amount of money, Spanish or foreign, that you may import. Departing, you should declare sums over the equivalent of 1,000,000 ptas.

Currency restrictions. Visitors may bring up to one million pesetas into or out of the country without a declaration. If you intend to bring in and take out larger sums, declare this on arrival and departure.

I have nothing to declare.   **No tengo nada a declarar.**

D

DRIVING

Crossing the border into Spain, you won't be asked for documents, but in the event of any problem you will have to produce a passport, a valid driver's license, proper registration papers, and a "Green Card" extension of your regular car insurance to make it valid in foreign countries. This can be obtained from your insurance company.

If you can avoid driving in Madrid, do so. Nerve-wracking traffic jams are a way of life. If not, try to drive between 3:30 and 4:30 p.m., when there is some lull in the traffic. Be careful late at night—there are many accidents on the streets in the early hours, when the clubs close. Madrid drivers are not noted for their courtesy.

Road Conditions. Roads within Madrid are very congested. Roads and highways (*autopistas*) outside of the capital are uniformly excellent.

Rules and Regulations. Your car should display a nationality sticker. Most fines for traffic offenses are payable on the spot. Driving rules are the same as throughout Spain: drive on the right, overtake (pass) on the left, yield right of way to vehicles coming from the right (unless your road is marked as having priority). Front and rear seat belts are compulsory. Speed limits are 120 km/h (75 mph) on motorways, 100 km/h (62 mph) on broad main roads (two lanes each way), 90 km/h (56mph) on other main roads, 50 km/h (31 mph), or as marked, in densely populated areas. Spaniards routinely appear to disregard speed limits, but that doesn't mean you should.

The roads are patrolled by the Traffic Civil Guard (*Guardia Civil de Tráfico*) on motorcycles. Courteous and helpful, they are also tough on lawbreakers. Fines are payable on the spot. Beware of drinking and driving. The permitted blood-alcohol level is low and penalties stiff.

Fuel Costs. Service stations are plentiful throughout Madrid and Castile. *Petrol* (gasoline) comes in 95 (Euro super lead-free), 97 (super) and 98 (lead-free super plus) grades, but not all at every station. Diesel fuel is widely available.

Parking. If driving in Madrid sometimes resembles a bad dream, parking is a positive nightmare. For many places, non-residents can buy parking tickets from a tobacconist or newsstand. The price—modest—depends on length of stay intended, and different colors indicate different lengths of stay (maximum 1 1/2 hours; any excess heavily fined). To make things worse, it's very often impossible to know if one is in such a zone (signposts are not easy comprehensible) so the only way to be sure is to ask. And it's worth doing so: even tourists' cars don't always escape the *grua* (tow-truck) that hauls away cars badly parked, and more than one tourist has returned to find a parking fine, held down by a stone, in the place where his car used to be. The simplest solution is usually to find the nearest underground parking area — more expensive but less complicated — and there are many of them.

Madrid

If You Need Help. Garages are efficient, but repairs may take time in busy tourist areas. Spare parts are readily available for Spanish-built cars and many other popular models. For less-common makes, they may have to be imported. For emergencies, dial tel. 091.

Road signs. Most signs are the standard pictographs used throughout Europe. However, you may encounter the following written signs in Spanish.

¡Alto!	Stop!
Aparcamiento	Parking
Autopista	Motorway
Ceda el paso	Give way (yield)
Cruce peligroso	Dangerous crossroads
Curva peligrosa	Dangerous bend
Despacio	Slow
Peligro	Danger
Prohibido adelantar	No overtaking (passing)
Prohibido aparcar	No parking

Car registration papers	**Permiso de circulación**
Are we on the right road for…?	**¿Es ésta la carretera hacia…?**
Full tank, please.	**Lléne el depósito, por favor.**
normal/super/unleaded	**normal/super/sin plomo**
Please check the oil/tires/battery.	**Por favor, controle el aceite/los neumáticos/la batería.**
Can I park here?	**¿Se puede aparcar aquí?**
My car has broken down.	**Mi coche se ha estropeado.**
There's been an accident.	**Ha habido un accidente.**

(International) Driving License **Carnet de conducir (internacional)**

Car-registration papers **Permiso de circulación**

Green card **Tarjeta verde**

E

ELECTRICITY *(corriente eléctrica)*
The standard is 220 volts, but some hotels have a voltage of 110–120 in bathrooms as a safety precaution. Check before plugging in any appliance.

Sockets (outlets) take round, two-pin plugs, so you will probably need an international adapter plug. Visitors from North America will need a transformer unless they have dual-voltage travel appliances.

What's the voltage? **¿Cuál es el voltaje?**

an adapter/a battery **un transformador/una pila/ una batería**

EMBASSIES/CONSULATES/HIGH COMMISSIONS *(embajadas; consulados)*
Almost all Western European countries have embassies that are located in Madrid.

Australia: Paseo de la Castellana, 143; Tel. 91/579 04 28

Canada: Núñez de Balboa, 35; Tel. 91/431 43 00

Ireland: Claudio Coello, 73; Tel. 91/576 35 00

New Zealand: Plaza de la Lealtad, 2; Tel. 91/523 02 26

South Africa: Claudio Coello, 91; Tel. 91/435 66 88

UK: Fernando el Santo, 16; Tel. 91/319 02 00

USA: Serrano, 75; Tel. 91/577 40 00

Citizens of Commonwealth countries may apply to the UK embassy.

Madrid

Where's the…embassy?	**¿Dónde está la embajada…?**
American/Australian/British/ Canadian/Irish/South African	**americana/australiana/británica/ canadiense/irlandesa/ sudafricana**

EMERGENCIES (*urgencias*) (see also Consulates, Medical Care, Police)

If your hotel receptionist isn't handy to help, and you have a real crisis, dial the police emergency number, 091.

Here are a few other numbers for urgent matters:

Fire	080
Ambulance	092
Accidents (municipal police)	092

Careful!	**¡Cuidado!**
Police!	**¡Policía!**
Fire!	**¡Fuego!**
Stop!	**¡Deténgase!**
Help!	**¡Socorro!**
Stop thief!	**¡Alto! ¡Ladrón!**

G

GAY AND LESBIAN TRAVELERS (*homosexual; gay*; *lesbiana*)

Madrid has Spain's most active and open gay community, and scores of clubs and nightlife options. Still, Conservative Catholic beliefs predominate in some sectors, so gay visitors may wish to be discrete. The area around Plaza de Chueca is where much gay nightlife is centered; Café Figueroa (Augusto Figueroa, 17) is one of the longtime pillars of gay life in the capital. For information, contact the **Coordinadora Gay de Madrid** (c/ Espíritu Santo, 37; Tel. 91/523 00 70). Look for the free magazines *Shangay Express,* and *Revista*

Mensual, available at kiosks, both of which have information and listings of clubs, restaurants and other entertainment options.

GETTING THERE (See also AIRPORT and DRIVING)

Air Travel (See also AIRPORTS on page 99)
Madrid's airport is linked by regularly scheduled daily non-stop flights from across Europe. Most flights from the US and Canada are direct; others stop first in Lisbon. From Australia and New Zealand, regular one-stop flights go directly to Madrid. Flying times: London, about 2 hours; New York, approximately six hours. Iberia, the Spanish national airline, covers most countries in shared arrangements with their own carriers.

A regular air shuttle connects Madrid and Barcelona. From points in Spain, there are many regularly scheduled flights to Madrid from virtually every city, on Iberia, Air Europa, and Spanair.

International Airport. Madrid's international airport is Barajas (Tel 91/393 60 00 or 91/305 83 43), 15 km (9 miles) east of Madrid.

Charter Flights and Package Tours: From the U.K. and Ireland, many companies operate comprehensive package tours, which include flight, hotel, and meals; check carefully to make sure that you are not liable to any surcharges. British travel agents offer guarantees in case of bankruptcy or cancellation by hotels or airlines. Most recommend insurance, too, for tourists who are forced to cancel because of illness or accident.

If you prefer to arrange your own accommodation and do not mind having to restrict your holiday to either one or two weeks, you can take advantage of the many charter flights that are available.

From North America, package tours including hotel, car, or other land arrangements can be a very good value. In addition to APEX and Excursion fares, there's the Advance Booking Charter (ABC), which must be bought at least 30 days in advance. Many retired people take advantage of special rates early and late in the year.

Madrid

By Road

The main access road from France to Madrid is at the western side of the Pyrenees. A motorway (expressway) runs from Biarritz (France) via Bilbao to Burgos, from where you take the E25 motorway straight down to Madrid, 240 km (150 miles) away.

Express **coach services** operate between London and Madrid as well as between other European cities and Madrid. You can also travel by coach as part of a package holiday.

By Rail

The overnight *tren hotel* (train hotel) Francisco de Goya operates between Madrid and Paris, and takes about 11 hours.

Rail passes: The *Eurailpass*, *Eurail Flexipass*, *Eurail Saverpass*, *Eurail Youthpass, Eurail Saver Flexipass,* and *Eurail Youth Flexipass* are valid for travel in Spain, but must be purchased outside Europe. They are not available for residents of Europe, the C.I.S., Turkey, or North Africa. Supplements must be paid for many high-speed or overnight trains. The *Spain Flexipass* is available for any 3 days in two months. The *Spain Rail 'n Drive* is available for any 5 days (3 rail and 2 car) within two months, and additional rail and car days are available. *Inter-Rail Pass*, *Freedom Pass* (for travellers under 26), and *Inter-Rail 26+ Pass* are valid for travel in Spain and most major European countries, and are available to residents of Europe.

Travel is cheaper on the off-peak days or *días azules*. For long distance (*Largo Recorrido*), train fares are based on the number of kilometers to be traveled and the expected volume of traffic on each train. Accordingly, each train is rated as either *Valle, Llano,* or *Punta*, with *Valle* being the cheapest and *Punta* the most expensive.

GUIDES AND TOURS *(guía; visitas guiadas)*

The Patronato Municipal de Turismo (City Tourism Office) offers historical and cultural tours by bus and by foot throughout the year, covering a wide array of topics and sights; ask at any tourism office about the **Discover Madrid** program and scheduled visits or call 91/588 29 06. Unless there's a large English-speaking group, though, tours are in Spanish. **Madrid Visión** (Tel. 91/302 45 26) organizes hop-on, hop-off multi-language city bus tours that depart from Gran Vía, 32.

Bus excursions to the major sights outside of Madrid — Aranjuez, El Escorial, Toledo, Ávila and Segovia—are arranged by three major players. Contact: **Juliatur** (Gran Vía, 68; Tel. 91/559 96 05; Metro: Plaza de España); **Pullmantur** (Plaza de Oriente, 8; Tel. 91/541 18 05; Metro: Ópera); or **Trapsatur** (San Bernardo, 23; Tel. 91/541 63 20; Metro: Santo Domingo).

We'd like an English-speaking guide.	**Queremos una guía que hable inglés.**
I need an English interpreter.	**Necesito un intérprete de inglés.**

H

HEALTH AND MEDICAL CARE

Standards of hygiene are high, and medical care in Madrid is generally excellent. Most doctors speak sufficient English to deal with foreign patients. The water is safe to drink, but bottled water is always safest, and is available everywhere. Even most local people drink bottled water, *agua con gas* (carbonated) or *sin gas* (still). It is good, clean, and inexpensive.

Visitors from E.U. countries with corresponding health-insurance facilities are entitled to medical and hospital treatment under the Spanish social security system. Before leaving home, ensure that you are eligible and have the appropriate forms. It is recommended that you take out reputable private medical insurance, which will be part of almost all travel insurance packages.

Pharmacies *(farmacias)* operate as a first line of defense for Spaniards, as pharmacists can prescribe drugs and are usually adept at making on-the-spot diagnoses. Pharmacies operate during normal business hours but there is always one in every district that remains open all night and on holidays. The location and phone number of this *farmacia de guardia* is posted on the door of all the other pharmacies. All-night pharmacies can also be contacted by calling 098. To locate a hospital or report a medical emergency, dial 112.

Where's the nearest (all-night) pharmacy?	**¿Dónde está la farmacia (de guardia) más cercana?**
I need a doctor/dentist.	**Necesito un médico/dentista.**
an ambulance/hospital	**una ambulancia/un hospital**
I've a pain here.	**Me duele aquí.**

HOLIDAYS *(fiestas)*

1 January	*Año Nuevo*	New Year's Day
6 January	*Epifanía*	Epiphany
20 January	*San Sebastián*	St. Sebastian's Day
1 May	*Día del Trabajo*	Labor Day
25 July	*Santiago Apóstol*	St. James's Day
15 August	*Asunción*	Assumption
12 October	*Día de la Hispanidad*	Discovery of America Day (Columbus Day)
1 November	*Todos los Santos*	All Saints' Day
6 December	*Día de la Española*	Constitution Day
25 December	*Navidad*	Christmas Day
26 December	*La Fiesta Navidad*	Christmas Holiday

Movable dates:

Jueves Santo	Holy Thursday
Viernes Santo	Good Friday

Lunes de Pascua	Easter Monday
Corpus Christi	Corpus Christi
Inmaculada Concepción	Immaculate Conception (normally 8 December)

In addition to these nation-wide holidays, Madrid celebrates May 2, as well as its patron saint's day—San Isidro Labrador (St. Isidore the Husbandman) on May 15—and *La Almudena* on November 9 as legal holidays.

LANGUAGE

After Chinese and English, the most widely spoken language in the world is Spanish—from Madrid to Manila, from Ávila to Argentina. The Castilian spoken in Madrid (seat of the all-powerful Royal Spanish Academy of the Language) is understood wherever you may travel in Spain.

French, English, and German are understood mainly in large international hotels and tourist-oriented establishments. The younger generation may speak English elsewhere, but it is certainly worth learning a few basic phrases.

English	**Castilian**
Good morning	*Buenos días*
Good afternoon	*Buenas tardes*
Good night	*Buenas noches*
Thank you	*Gracias*
You're welcome	*De nada*
Please	*Por favor*
Goodbye	*Adiós*
Welcome	*Bienvenido*
See you later	*Hasta luego*

Madrid

Hello	*Hola*
Nice to meet you.	*Encantado de conocerle.*
Do you speak English?	*¿Habla inglés?*
I don't understand.	*No entiendo.*

Additional Phrases

yes/no	**sí/no**
excuse me/you're welcome	**perdone/de nada**
where/when/how	**dónde/cuándo/cómo**
yesterday/today/tomorrow	**ayer/hoy/mañana**
day/week/month/year	**día/semana/mes/año**
left/right/up/down	**izquierda/derecha/arriba/abajo**
good/bad	**bueno/malo**
big/small	**grande/pequeño**
hot/cold	**caliente/frío**
old/new	**viejo/nuevo**
open/closed	**abierto/cerrado**
early/late	**temprano/tarde**
What does this mean?	**¿Qué quiere decir esto?**
Please write it down.	**Escríbamelo, por favor.**
Is there an admission charge?	**¿Se debe pagar la entrada?**
I'd like…	**Quisiera…**
How much is that?	**¿Cuánto es?**
Help me, please.	**Ayúdeme, por favor.**
Get a doctor quickly!	**¡Llamen a un médico, rápidamente.**

The Berlitz *Spanish Phrasebook and Dictionary* covers all situations you are likely to encounter in your travels in Spain. It contains a 12,500-word glossary of each language, plus a helpful menu-reader supplement.

MAPS

Free street maps covering the whole of Madrid are available at Tourist Information Offices at the airport, train stations and in the city (see Tourist Information, p. 123). It is sufficient for virtually all city travel. Visitors should also pick up the pocket-sized map of the Metro subway system, available free at any Metro station.

MEDIA *(periódico; revista)*

Most European, including British and German, newspapers are sold on the day of publication, as are the Paris-based *International Herald Tribune* and European edition of *The Wall Street Journal*. *USA Today* is also widely available, as are principal European and American magazines. All of these can be found at the many kiosks along Gran Vía or near Puerta del Sol. For Spanish-speakers or those willing to give it a try, the weekly entertainment information magazine *Guía del Ocio* (Leisure Guide) lists bars, restaurants, cinema, theater, and concerts.

Most hotels and bars have television, usually tuned to sports (international or local), and broadcasting in Spanish. Satellite dishes are sprouting, and most tourist hotels offer multiple channels (German, French, Sky, BBC, CNN, Super, etc.). Reception of Britain's BBC World Service radio is usually good to excellent. A good set will receive the BBC long-wave and even medium-wave domestic programs.

Where's a newspaper kiosk? **¿Dónde hay un kiosco?**

Have you any English-language newspapers/magazines? **¿Tienen periódicos/revistas en inglés?**

Madrid

MONEY (*dinero; efectivo*)

Currency (*moneda*). The monetary unit of Spain is the *peseta* (abbreviated *pta.* and occasionally *ptas.*). Coins in circulation are 1, 5, 10, 25, 50, 100, 200, and 500 pta. Banknotes are available in denominations of 1,000, 2,000, 5,000, and 10,000 pta.

The *Euro* remains an electronic/banking currency until 1 January 2002, when it will be introduced in the form of bills and coins. After a six-month transition period, on 1 July 2002, the Euro will become Spain's single currency.

Currency exchange. Banks are the best place to exchange currency, offering the best rates with no commission. Many travel agencies and *casas de cambio* (displaying a *cambio* sign) will also exchange foreign currency into pesetas and stay open outside banking hours. However, be wary of those advertising "no commission." (Their rates are much lower, so you are in effect paying a hefty commission.) Both banks and exchange offices pay slightly more for traveler's checks than for cash. Always take your passport when you go to change money, as you will frequently be requested to present it. Outside banking hours, you may use exchange offices (*cambio*) at Chamartín railway station, Gran Vía/Callao (open 24 hours), the airport or your own hotel.

Credit cards (*tarjetas de crédito*). Major international cards are widely recognized, though smaller businesses tend to prefer cash. Cards linked to Visa/Eurocard/MasterCard are most generally accepted. They are also useful for obtaining cash advances from banks. A credit card will usually give you the highest exchange rate, translated at the time of billing rather than the moment of transaction.

ATMs. Cash machines are now ubiquitous in Spain. They dispense currency in pesetas—usually multiples of 5,000.

Traveler's Checks. (*cheques de viajero*). Hotels, shops, restaurants, and travel agencies all cash traveler's checks, and so do banks, where you're likely to get a better rate (you will need your passport). Since you have to pay for them (often 1-2% of their value), traveler's checks are less desirable than a combination of credit cards and ATM machines. Try to cash small amounts at a time, keeping some of your holiday funds in checks, in the hotel safe. In addition, you'll have no problem settling bills with Eurocheques, provided you have the Eurocheque cash card.

Where's the nearest bank /currency exchange office?	**¿Dónde está el banco/ la casa de cambio más cercana?**
I want to change some pounds/dollars.	**Quiero cambiar libras/ dólares.**
Do you accept traveler's checks?	**¿Aceptan cheques de viajero?**
Can I pay with a credit card?	**¿Se puede pagar con tarjeta?**
How much is that?	**¿Cuánto es/vale?**

OPEN HOURS

The practice of the siesta, the long midday break and nap, is losing adherents in Madrid, the busy capital. The big department stores and grocery stores remain open all day and factories also work full shifts. Still, very few shops remain open all day; usual hours are from 9:30am–1:30pm or 2pm and 4:30pm-5pm or 8 p.m. Monday– Saturday. Many museums and other tourist attractions maintain the same schedule.

Post offices are usually Monday–Friday 9am–2pm, Saturday 9am–1pm. **Banks** generally open Monday–Friday 8:30/9am–2:30pm (1:30pm in summer), Saturdays 9am–1pm (except summer). **Restaurants** serve lunch from 1pm–4pm. In the evenings their timing depends on the kind of customers they expect. Locals usually eat between 8:30 and 11pm or later. Places catering to foreigners may function from 7pm on, and many stay open throughout the day.

Madrid

Government offices and the vast majority of businesses are open from 9am–2pm and from 3pm to anywhere from 5:30–7pm.

P

POLICE *(policía)*

Spanish municipal and national police are efficient, strict, and courteous—and generally very responsive to issues involving foreign tourists. In Madrid, dial 092 for municipal police and 091 for national police. The main police station (Policía Nacional) is located at calle Fomento, 24, near Plaza de España (Tel. 91/541 7160).

Where's the nearest police station?	**¿Dónde está la comisaría más cercana?**

POST OFFICES *(correos)*

Post offices handle mail and telegrams, but not normally telephone calls. Post Offices — all identified by yellow-and-white signs with a crown and the words "Correos y Telégrafos" — in Spain are for mail and telegrams; you can't usually telephone from them. The postal system has greatly improved in recent years and is now generally pretty reliable. Opening hours are usually 9am–2pm Monday–Friday, 9am–1pm Saturday. The Central Post Office is located at Palacio de Comunicaciones, Plaza de la Cibeles (Tel 91/537 64 94). It's open Monday–Friday, 8:30am–9pm and Saturday from 8am–8pm. Branches of the Post Office are identified by the yellow sign "Correos." Most post office branches are open from 9 am–2pm (some services only until 1 o'clock or earlier).

Stamps *(sellos)* can be purchased at the post office or at *estancos* (tobacconist stands — look for the brown-and-yellow sign that reads "Tabacos"). Rates are divided into four areas of the world, just like telephone calls: the EU, rest of Europe, the US and Canada, and the rest of the world. Airmail letters to the United States and Canada cost 115 pta. up to 20 grams, and letters to Britain or other EU countries cost 65 ptas. up to 20 grams. Postcards have the same rates as letters. Allow about one week for delivery to North America, and 4-5 days to the UK. To speed things up, send a letter *urgente* express) or *certificado* (registered).

Where is the Post Office?	**¿Dónde está el Correos?**
A stamp for this letter/ postcard, please.	**Por favor, un sello para esta carta/tarjeta postal.**
I'd like to send this letter.	**Me gustaría enviar esta carta.**
airmail	**vía aérea**
express (special delivery)	**urgente**
registered	**certificado**
How long will it take to arrive?	**¿Cuánto tarda en llegar?**

PUBLIC TRANSPORTATION

Madrid has a reliable and comprehensive public transport system; getting around town, especially by Metro (subway/tube) is easy, rapid, and inexpensive. Collect an up-to-date bus and train timetable from the tourist information office or any Metro station.

By Bus (*autobús*). The municipal transportation system, EMT, operates bus routes criss-crossing Madrid. Municipal buses operate from 6am–12am (night buses called "buhos" operate from midnight–6am, but much less frequently). A bargain ticket *(Bono Bus)*, valid for ten rides, is available at EMT booths and in the savings banks (Caja Madrid).

By Metro (subway): Madrid's underground (subway) system combines speed with economy. For the Metro, too, there is a cheaper 10-ride ticket *(billete de diez viajes)*, 705 ptas. The Metro runs daily from 6am–1:30am. Good pocket-sized maps are available at Metro stations.

By Taxi. Madrid's 15,000 taxis are easily recognized by the letters *SP* (for *servicio público*, or public service) on front and rear bumpers. Madrid taxis are white with a red stripe. If a taxi is free, a *libre* ("free") sign is displayed in the windshield. The meter shows an initial charge at the drop of the flag. The figure displayed at the end of your trip may not be the full price. Legitimate added charges are compounded for night and holiday travel, airport pickups, etc. Non-metered tourist cars, which often solicit business at major hotels and nightclubs, charge premium rates. If you need to call a cab, taxi companies include **Tele-Taxi** (Tel. 91/445 90 08), **Radio Teléfono Taxi** (Tel. 91/547 82 00) and **Radio Taxi Independiente** (Tel. 91/405 12 13). Check the fare before you get in; rates are fixed and are displayed in several languages on the window. Also ensure that the meter has been reset when you begin your journey. Refuse a cab if the driver claims the meter is not working.

By Train *(tren)*: Madrid divides train service among three stations. Atocha (Glorieta del Emperador Carlos V; Metro: Atocha RENFE; Tel. 91/328 90 20) is the station for destinations in south and southeast Spain and Portugal. The high-speed AVE train departs for (and arrives from) Córdoba and Seville at Atocha; Tel. 91/534 05 05 or Tel. 91/328 90 20. Charmartín (calle Agustín de Foxá; Metro: Charmartín), the most modern train station, covers most destinations in north and northeastern Spain, in addition to most European capitals. Estación Príncipe Pío (also called "Estación Norte"; Paseo del Norte, 30; Metro: Norte; Tel. 91/328/90 20) is the station for trains to and from northwestern Spain, including Salamanca and Galicia.

 RENFE is the Spanish national train service; its main office, open weekdays only, is located at Alcalá, 44 (Metro: Banco de España; Tel. 91/328 90 20).

When's the next bus/train to…?	**¿Cuándo sale el próximo autobús/tren para…?**
bus station	**estación de autobuses**
A ticket to…	**Un billete para…**
single (one-way)	**ida**
return (round-trip)	**ida y vuelta**
What's the fare to…?	**¿Cuánto es la tarifa a …?**

R

RELIGION (*religión; servicios religiosos*)
The national religion of Spain is Roman Catholicism, and Mass is said regularly in the churches of Madrid, great and small. There are churches of most major faiths; the tourist information offices (see below) have information on religious services, including those in foreign languages.

T

TELEPHONE

Spain's country code is 34. Madrid's local area code, 91, must be dialed before all phone numbers, even for local calls. The telephone office is independent of the post office and is identified by a blue and white sign. You can make direct-dial local and international calls from public telephone booths (*cabinas*) in the street. Most operate with both coins and cards; international telephone credit cards can also be used. Instructions for use are given in several languages in the booths, which are widely distributed throughout the islands. Pick up the receiver and when you get the dial tone, dial 01; wait for a second dial tone to enter (the country code), local code, and the number you are calling.

Madrid's main telephone offices (Teléfonicas) are located at: Gran Vía/Fuencarral (Metro: Gran Via) and Paseo de Recoletos, 41 (Metro: Colón). These are open from 9am to midnight, Monday–Saturday and from 10am–midnight on Sundays and feast days. The main post office also has a communications center with international phone, telex, and fax services. It is open from 8am–midnight during the week and 8 am–10pm on weekends.

You can also make calls at public telephone offices called *locutorios*. These are much quieter than making a call on the street, and a clerk will place the call for you. You pay for the call afterwards.

Local, national and international calls can also be made from hotels, but almost always with an exorbitant surcharge. You are wise to make these with an international calling card, if you must make them from your hotel room. (Before departure, be sure to get the international access code in Spain for your long distance telephone carrier at home.)

For most calls, including international calls, at pay phones, it's wise to use a phone card (*tarjeta telefónica*), which can be purchased in 1,000-pta. and 2,000-pta. versions at any *estanco* (tobacconist shop; look for the sign "Tabacos"). Calls are cheaper after 10pm and after 2pm on Saturday and all day Sunday.

Phone booths have instructions in English for making collect and operator-assisted calls.

If you wish to send a fax, you may do so from most hotels, though the charge can be as high as US $5 per page. Fax machines for public use can be found in communication centers in most holiday resorts.

Can you get me this number in…?	**¿Puede comunicarme con este número en…?**

TIME ZONES

Spanish time coincides with most of Western Europe—Greenwich Mean Time plus one hour. In spring, another hour is added for Daylight Saving Time (Summer Time).

Summer Time chart:

New York	London	**Madrid**	Jo'burg	Sydney	Auckland
6 a.m.	11 a.m.	**noon**	noon	8 p.m.	10 p.m

What time is it?	**¿Qué hora es?**

TIPPING (*propina; servicio*)

Since a service charge is normally included in hotel and restaurant bills, tipping is not obligatory. However, it's normal to leave a small coin (about 5% of the bill) after service at a bar counter, and 5-10% on restaurant bills. Taxi drivers do not need to be tipped unless one gives you special service. Additional guidelines:

Hotel porter, per bag	100 pta.

Lavatory attendant	25-50 pta.
Tour guide	10%

Is service (tip) included?	**¿Está incluido el servicio?**

TOILETS

There are many expressions for "toilets" in Spanish: *aseos, lavabos, servicios,* and *W.C.* The first two are the most common. Toilet doors are distinguished by a "C" for "*Caballeros*" (gentlemen) or "S" for "*Señoras*" (ladies) or by a variety of pictographs.

In addition to the well-marked public toilets in the main squares and stations, a number of neat coin-operated toilets in portable cabins marked "W.C." are installed at convenient locations around the city. Just about every bar and restaurant has a toilet available for public use. It is considered polite to buy a drink if you drop in specifically to use the conveniences.

Where are the toilets?	**¿Dónde están los servicios?**

TOURIST INFORMATION *(oficinas de información turística)*

Spanish National Tourist Offices are maintained in many countries:

Australia: International House, Suite 44, 104 Bathurst St, P.O. Box A-675, 2000 Sydney NSW; Tel. (02) 264 79 66

Canada: 62 Bloor St. West, Suite 3402, Toronto, Ontario M4W 3E2; Tel. (1416) 961-3131

U.K.: 22-23 Manchester Square, London W1M 5AP; Tel. (171) 486-8077

U.S.A.: Water Tower Place, Suite 915 East, 845 North Michigan Ave, Chicago, IL 60611; Tel. (312) 944-0216/642-1992

8383 Wilshire Blvd, Suite 960, 90211 Beverly Hills, CA 90211; Tel. (213) 658-7188

666 5th Ave, 35th floor, New York, NY 10103; Tel. (212) 265-8822

1221 Brickell Ave., Ste. 1850, Miami, FL 33131; Tel. (305) 358-1992

Madrid

Key phone numbers:

General Madrid information: Tel. 901/300 600.

Telephone tourism information: Tel. 902/20 22 02 or 901/30 16 00.

General telephone information: Tel. 098.

National telephone information: Tel. 009.

Tourist information offices in Madrid:

Municipal Tourism Offices are located at Plaza Mayor, 3 (Tel. 91/366 54 77); Duque de Medinaceli, 2 (Tel. 91/429 49 51); Puerta de Toledo Market, 1-6 (Tel. 91/364 18 75); and Barajas Airport (International Arrivals Terminal; Tel. 91/305 86 56).

Where is the tourist office?   **¿Dónde está la oficina de turismo?**

WEB SITES & INTERNET ACCESS

The Internet is a good place for those who are wired to get information before they go. Check <www.tourspain.es>, the helpful, up-to-date official site of Turespaña, the National Tourism Office. Also helpful is <www.munimadrid.es>, Madrid Tourism Office's web page.

There are several internet cafes and computer centers in Madrid where visitors can go to access the Internet and e-mail. *WWW.call.home* near Plaza San Andrés (Plaza Puerta de Moros, 2; Tel. 91/354 01 04), open daily, offers both reduced-rate international telephone calls and internet access. Other internet access providers include: Amiweb (c/ Mayor, 4–Piso 4/Oficina 8; Tel. 91/532 08 21) and La Casa de Internet (c/Luchana, 20-1; Tel. 91/446 55 41).

WEIGHTS AND MEASURES

Spain uses the metric system.

Distance

km	0	1	2	3	4	5	6	8	10	12	14	16
miles	0	½	1	1½	2		3	4	5	6	7	8	9	10

Length

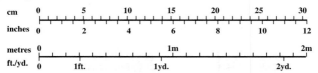

Weight

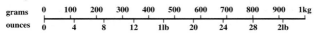

Temperature

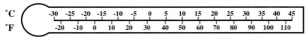

Fluid measures

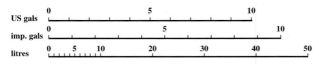

Y

YOUTH HOSTELS

There are several inexpensive hotels in Madrid and the surrounding area, but youth hostels are also an option. In Madrid, Alburgue Juvenil Marcenado (Santa Cruz de Marcenado, 28; Tel. 91/547 45 32; fax 91/548 11 96; 72 beds), or Albergue Juvenil Casa de Campo (Tel. 91/463 56 99; fax 91/464 46 85; 130 beds). In Toledo, Residencia Juvenil San Sevando (Castillo San Servando; Tel. 925/22 45 54; 46 beds).

Recommended Hotels

Madrid, long one of Spain's top tourist destinations, is swarming with hotels, many of them populated by business travelers and large tour groups. Most traditional hotels are either located in Old and Bourbon Madrid, especially around the Gran Vía, a well-communicated area but one that is exceedingly busy and potentially noisy; newer accommodations are found in the residential neighborhoods beyond the center. Visitors have plenty of choices, from cheap *pensiones* and *residencias* to ultra-deluxe palaces, but accommodations in Madrid are more expensive than any other city in Spain, including Barcelona.

Weekend rates and special deals are available at many hotels. Most hotel rates do not include either breakfast or IVA, the 7% value-added tax. Be sure to ask about these. Since a large portion of Madrid's hotels cater to business travelers, weekend rates and special deals are available at many hotels — always ask. Unless it's high season and the hotel's near capacity, you'll probably get a break.

Overnight stays are the best ways to enjoy several of the spectacular cities of Castile outside Madrid, particularly Segovia and Toledo. National paradors are state-owned and -operated hotels, often in renovated historic buildings, that usually offer excellent service and luxury standards for a reasonable price.

The following guide indicates rack-rate prices for a double room in high season (Prices should be used as an approximate guide only):

$$$$$	above 25,000 ptas.
$$$$	18,000-25,000 ptas.
$$$	12,000–18,000 ptas.
$$	7,500–12,000 ptas.
$	under 7,500 ptas.

Old Madrid/Puerta del Sol

Hostal Lisboa $ *Ventura de la Vega, 17; Tel. 91/429 98 94; fax 91/369 41 96.* Madrid is littered with small, affordable *residencias* (pensions), and this is one of the best bargains among them. Rooms are comfortably large, with a small sitting area, and bathrooms are surprisingly spacious. 27 rooms. Major credit cards.

Hotel Inglés $$ *calle Echegaray, 8; Tel. 91/429 65 51; fax 91/420 24 23.* A slightly upscale version of an *hostal* or *pensión*, the "English Hotel" is well located, about equidistant from the Prado and the Plaza Mayor. The lobby outclasses the somewhat plain rooms, but they are comfortable and economical. Wheelchair access. 58 rooms. Major credit cards.

Hotel Paris $$ *calle de Alcalá 2; Tel. 91/521 64 91; fax 91/531 01 88.* A simple but charming Old World hotel just paces from the Puerta del Sol. The place has lots of Bohemian flavor befitting the name. Rooms are comfortable, if a tad gloomy. Regulars have shown up yearly for decades. Wheelchair access. 121 rooms. Major credit cards.

Suite Prado Hotel $$$$ *calle Manuel Fernández y González, 10; Tel. 91/420 23 18; fax 91/420 05 59.* The price may look a little steep, until you realize that all the brightly decorated rooms are suites large enough to get lost in, with unheard-of kitchenettes and comfortable salons for the price of a standard three- or four-star room. It's just minutes from the Plaza Mayor and the Prado. Small and in demand, so make reservations several weeks in advance. Wheelchair access. 18 rooms. Major credit cards.

Tryp Reina Victoria $$$$$ *Plaza Santa Ana, 14; Tel. 91/531 45 00; Fax 91/522 03 07; e-mail <hotel@tryp.es>.* A historic 1920s hotel on animated Plaza Santa Ana, this old favorite was once a hangout of bullfighters (who are paid tribute to in the clubby bar). Rooms are spacious and classically decorated; some views of the (noisy) plaza. Wheelchair access. 200 rooms. Major credit cards.

Old Madrid/Gran Vía–Plaza de España

Hotel Arosa $$$-$$$$ *calle Salud, 21 (Edificio Gran Vía, 29); Tel. 91/532 16 00; fax 91/531 31 27.* A very elegant, well-run hotel just steps from Gran Vía, but insulated to keep the noise out. With handsome rooms and a very comfortable lobby, the hotel feels more intimate than its large size would indicate. Ideally located if you want to see a lot of Madrid in a short time. A Best Western hotel. Wheelchair access. 140 rooms. Major credit cards.

Hotel Santo Domingo $$$$-$$$$$ *Plaza Santo Domingo 13; Tel. 91/547 98 00; fax 91/547 59 95; web site* <www.stnet.es/hotel_domingo>. Close to the heart of Old Madrid, this 1994 hotel is surprisingly personal and elegant, despite the somewhat chaotic plaza it sits on. Rooms are classically decorated and warm. Rooms vary significantly in size and layout. A Best Western hotel. Wheelchair access. 120 rooms. Major credit cards.

Tryp Ambassador $$$$$ *Cuesta Santo Domingo 5-7; Tel. 91/541 67 00; fax 91/559 10 40.* This handsome hotel, opened about a decade ago near the Royal Palace, occupies a magnificent palace and converted monastery, both meticulously renovated. The hotel is on a quiet, sloping old street near Viejo Madrid's principal attractions. Rooms are large and sophisticated. Wheelchair access. 181 rooms. Major credit cards.

Holiday Inn Crowne Plaza $$$$$ *Plaza de España, 8; Tel. 91/454 85 00; fax 91/548 23 89; web site* <www.crowneplaza .com>. This huge high-rise right on the Plaza de España is all sheen and international sophistication, but is not as elegant as one might think. The rooms facing the Plaza have excellent views of the Royal Palace, but at a wallet-emptying price. Wheelchair access. 306 rooms. Major credit cards.

Hotel Carlos V $$$ *Maestro Victoria, 5; Tel. 91/531 41 00; fax 531 37 61;* web site <www.bestwestern.com/thisco/ bw/92119_b.html>. The older-style "Carlos Quinto" is wedged in a pedestrian street between the Puerta del Sol and Gran Vía, an excellent location. Comfortable and affordable It's usually full but without the tour groups at most Gran Vía hotels. A Best Western hotel. Wheelchair access. 65 rooms. Major credit cards.

Hotel Príncipe Pío $$ *Cuesta de San Vicente, 16; Tel. 91/547 08 00; fax 541 11 17; e-mail* <hotelppio@futurnet.es>. Not far from the Campo del Moro and Royal Palace, this large hotel has a faded glory about it, but is a good value given its spectacular views of the Palacio Real and Manazares Valley. Old-style rooms are well maintained but plain. Seek a room on one of the upper floors, as the street is extremely busy and noisy. Wheelchair access. 185 rooms. Major credit cards.

Bourbon Madrid

Hotel NH Nacional $$$$ *Paseo del Prado, 48; Tel. 91/429 66 29; fax 91/369 15 64; web site* <www.nh-hoteles.es>. Spain's NH chain made its reputation designing commodious, professional, and efficient hotels for business travelers, but they're also ideal for many tourists. This one, opened in 1997 in a historic 1920s building, is right on museum mile, just a few paces from the Reina Sofía and a nice walk from the Prado. Wheelchair access. 214 rooms. Major credit cards.

Hotel Villa Real $$$$$ *Plaza de las Cortés, 10; Tel. 91/420 37 67; fax 91/420 25 47; web site* <www.derbyhotels.es>. A member of the small but excellent Derby chain of Barcelona hotels, this top-notch hotel is designed to compete with the Palace and Ritz just down the street. Installed in the mid-90s in a quasi-historic building, this traditional-minded hotel puts the emphasis on creature comforts, with plush rooms and bathrooms, but little pretense. Wheelchair access. 115 rooms. Major credit cards.

Hotel Ritz $$$$$ *Plaza de la Lealtad, 5; Tel. 800/225-5843 in the U.S. and Canada, or 91/521 28 57; fax 91/532 87 76; web site <www.ritz.es>.* In Madrid, the first and last word in elegance and sophistication. The turn-of-the-century hotel reeks of international glamour and clings to its formal (jacket and tie) ambience. Where aristocrats and movie stars and others who can afford it stay. Wheelchair access. 158 rooms. Major credit cards.

Palace Hotel $$$$$ *Plaza de las Cortés, 7; Tel. 800/325-3535 in the U.S., 800/325-3589 in Canada, or 91/360 80 00; fax 91/360 81 00; web site <www.ittsheraton.com>.* A beautiful Belle Époque hotel that's slightly less formal than the smaller Ritz, but every bit as stylish and elegant. The public areas are spectacular, the rooms a bit less so, but a long-awaited renovation was carried out in 1998. Right on the Paseo del Prado. Wheelchair access. 455 rooms. Major credit cards.

Hotel Mora $-$$ *Paseo del Prado, 32; Tel. 91/420 15 69; fax 91/420 05 64.* Down the street from the Prado and around the corner from the Reina Sofía museum, this well located hotel is a bargain. Rooms are rather plain, not nearly as impressive as the address or even the lobby, but they are more than functional. Busy cafeteria downstairs. Wheelchair access. 62 rooms. Major credit cards.

Hotel Mediodía $ *Plaza del Emperador Carlos V, 8; Tel. 91/527 30 60; fax 91/530 70 08.* In a grand old corner building across from the Atocha train station and seconds from the Reina Sofía contemporary art museum, this inexpensive hotel may have seen better days, but it remains a bargain. Wheelchair access. 165 rooms. Major credit cards.

Modern Madrid

Santo Mauro Hotel $$$$$ *calle Zurbano, 36; Tel. 91/319 69 00; fax 91/308 54 77*. This haven of design-oriented luxury, occupying a former palace and then embassy, is the place to be if you don't care for the old-money ambience and size of the Ritz and Palace. It's in a quiet residential neighborhood a mile or so from the old center, not nearly as convenient as its main competitors, but it offers uncommon intimacy and personal attention. Rooms are very chic, with full audio systems. Excellent restaurant. Wheelchair access. 37 rooms. Major credit cards.

Hotel Mónaco $$ *calle Barbieri, 5; Tel. 91/522 46 30; fax 91/521 16 01*. Madrid's funkiest hotel is this former brothel in the city's chief bohemian district. It's kitschy and cartoonish, with pink marble, neon lights, and faux-Louis XIV furniture. Rooms are all different, but singles are disappointingly plain. Wheelchair access. 34 rooms. Major credit cards.

Segovia

Hotel Infanta Isabel $$-$$$ *Plaza Mayor; Tel. 921/46 13 03; fax 921/46 22 17*. Perfectly located right on the central Plaza Mayor, this small 19th-century hotel is charming. Some of the large doubles have small terraces and picture-perfect views of the plaza and cathedral. Nice Victorian décor and great service — a bargain. Wheelchair access. 29 rooms. Major credit cards.

Hotel Los Linajes $$ *Dr. Velasco, 9; Tel. 921/46 04 75; fax 921/46 04 79*. A peaceful mid-size hotel on a side street in the San Esteban quarter, that feels perfectly in sync with old Segovia. Though much of it is new construction, other parts occupy a 17th-century palace that belonged to a noble Segovian family. Some rooms have priceless panoramic views. Renovated in 1999. Wheelchair access. 53 rooms. Major credit cards.

Parador de Segovia $$$$ *Ctra. de Valladolid, s/n; Tel. 921/44 37 37; fax 921/ 43 73 62; web site <www.parador.es>*. This airy and modern state-owned parador has breathtaking views of the magical outline of Segovia, including the Roman aqueduct, medieval walls, cathedral and castle (all illuminated at night). Perched on a hill 3 km/2 miles north of the city, it's less convenient than hotels in the old quarter, but perfect if you've got some time to relax in Segovia and aren't on a whirlwind tour of Castile. Wheelchair access. 113 rooms. Major credit cards.

Ávila

Hostería de Bracamonte $$ *Bracamonte, 6; Tel. 920/25 12 80; e-mail <bracamonte@estanciases.es>*. A small and tranquil, rustic hotel within the city walls. It occupies a 16th-century mansion, with thick stone walls and heavy wooden beams, and is decorated with excellent taste. Some rooms upstairs have fireplaces and four-poster beds. 20 rooms. Major credit cards.

Palacio de los Velada $$$ *Plaza de la Catedral, 10; Tel. 920/25 51 00; fax 920/25 49 00*. A surprisingly swank, handsomely restored 16th-century palace right across from the cathedral. Once frequented by royalty, it was converted into a hotel in 1995. Rooms are luxurious, and the hotel pub especially atmospheric. Excellent restaurant. Wheelchair access. 85 rooms. Major credit cards.

Parador de Ávila $$$ *Marques de Canales de Chozas, 2; Tel. 920/21 13 40; fax 920/22-61-66*. While this state-run parador convincingly updates a 16th-century palace downstairs, guest rooms are modern, though nicely outfitted. Just within Ávila's medieval walls. Wheelchair access. 60 rooms. Major credit cards.

Toledo

Hostal del Cardenal $$-$$$ *Paseo de Recaredo, 24; Tel. 925/22 08 62 (reservations, tel. 925/22 49 00); fax 925/22 29 91; e-mail <ciutod.direc@ac-hoteles.com>.* In the former residence of an 18th-century cardinal, this charming small hotel occupies part of the city's medieval fortifications. Its tranquil Moorish gardens with fountains and quiet patios are its main selling point, though rooms are very comfortable. Full most of the year, so make reservations early. Classic Castilian restaurant. 27 rooms. Major credit cards.

AC Hoteles Ciudad de Toledo $$$-$$$$ *Ctra. de Circunvalación, 15; Tel. 925/28 51 25; fax 925/28 47 00; e-mail <ciutod.direc@ac-hoteles.com>.* This new hotel has supplanted the national parador as the top choice in Toledo. Across the river from the city, it has superb views; rooms are very contemporary in design. It's part of the AC Hoteles family that includes the luxurious Santo Mauro in Madrid. Wheelchair access. 49 rooms. Major credit cards.

Hotel Pintor El Greco $$$ *Alamillos del Tránsito, 13; Tel. 925/21 42 50; fax 925/21 58 19; e-mail <elgreco@estanciases.es>.* Very Toledan in feel, this small hotel in a 17th-century noble home is named for the city's most famous (adopted) son. In the heart of the old Jewish quarter, it is very is peaceful and close to the El Greco museum and synagogues. Sunny rooms surround a central courtyard. Wheelchair access. 33 rooms. Major credit cards.

Parador de Toledo $$$-$$$$ *Cerro del Emperador, s/n; Tel. 925/22 18 50; fax 925/22 51 66; web site <www.parador.es>.* This is still the most popular hotel for groups. Very Castilian in feel, but the views from the terraces and large pool are the chief attractions. Reserve in advance. 77 rooms. Wheelchair access. Major credit cards.

Recommended Restaurants

Restaurant categories reflect a three-course meal: appetizer, main course and dessert. Many restaurants offer inexpensive fixed-priced menus (*menú del día, menú de la casa*), making lunch, the main meal of the day, surprisingly affordable. You can also assemble a meal by sharing a number of *raciones*—larger portions of tapas.

Locals eat lunch and dinner especially late (see page 117). You can either join them in the hunt for late-afternoon and early-evening tapas, staving off dinner, or go right when restaurants open, where foreigners are likely to be the only diners. (Most restaurants close between lunch and dinner. Those that do not are noted below.)

It's wise to make advance reservations, especially at the pricier establishments. The price guides below reflect the cost of an à la carte three-course meal for one with house wine. Gratuities are included in the meal price, but the 7% value-added-tax (IVA) will also be calculated into your final bill.

$$$$	above 6,000 ptas.
$$$	4,000-6,000 ptas.
$$	2,000-4,000 ptas.
$	under 2,000 ptas.

Old Madrid

Artemisa $-$$ *calle Tres Cruces, 4; Tel. 91/521 87 21.* A terrific-value vegetarian restaurant near Gran Vía serving creative dishes, like stuffed eggplant, with very fresh ingredients. The lunch *menú* is very popular with nearby office workers, so come before or after the 1:30pm–3pm rush. No smoking (a rarity in

Spain). A second branch is located at Ventura de la Vega, 4. Major credit cards.

Botín $$$-$$$$ *calle de Cuchilleros, 17; Tel. 91/366 42 17.* Open daily for lunch and dinner. Claimed to be oldest continuous restaurant in the world, having opened in 1725. That's old enough to have employed Francisco de Goya as a dishwasher before his talented hands gained fame for more artistic pursuits. Just beyond the Plaza Mayor, this is a classic Madrid restaurant tavern, swarming with tourists: roast suckling pig and roast leg of lamb prepared in wood ovens. Major credit cards.

Casa Alberto $$ *calle de las Huertas, 18; Tel. 91/429 93 56.* Open Tuesday–Saturday for lunch and dinner without interruption; Sunday, lunch only. A 1827 tavern where Cervantes once lived, this is a good place for a tapas and beer pulled from an antique tap in front, or a sit-down meal in back. The traditional choices include meatballs, cod stew, roasted lamb and ox. Major credit cards.

Casa Lucio $$$ *Cava Baja 35; Tel. 91/365 32 52.* Open Sunday–Friday lunch; dinner daily. Closed August. A historic cave-like tavern with hanging cured hams, popular with locals and visitors alike. High-quality Castilian cuisine like shrimp in garlic sauce and roasted lamb. Major credit cards.

Casa Paco $$$ *Puerta Cerrada, 11; Tel. 91/366 31 66.* Open Monday–Saturday, lunch and dinner. Closed August. A popular, 75-year-old steak house serving up thick slabs of beef, priced according to weight. The steaks are seared in oil and usually served very pink. Plenty of grilled fish dishes for non-meat-eaters. In the heart of Viejo Madrid. Major credit cards.

El Cosaco $$ *Plaza de la Paja, 2; Tel. 91/365 35 48.* Open: Sunday–Monday for dinner; Sunday, lunch and dinner. A reasonable and romantic Russian restaurant on one of the city's most serene plazas. The place to go when instead of roast suckling pig, you want blinis and vodka. Major credit cards.

El Schotis $$-$$$ *Cava Baja, 11; Tel. 91/365 32 20.* Open Monday–Saturday for lunch and dinner; Sunday for lunch only. A cozy little restaurant on an Old Madrid lined with friendly tascas. A good place for grilled meats (*churrasco*) or Basque-style fish dishes. Major credit cards.

La Bola $$$ *calle de la Bola, 5;. Tel. 91/547 69 30.* Open Monday–Saturday for lunch and dinner. A striking Madrid red corner bar, this old-school tavern has been around for 120 years. The house specialty is *cocido,* a stew they claim takes six hours to make. Also good grilled meats and fish. No credit cards.

La Posada de la Villa $$$-$$$$ *Cava Baja, 9; Tel. 91/366 18 60.* Open Monday–Saturday for lunch and dinner; Sunday, dinner only. Closed August. One of Viejo Madrid's best-looking, most authentic restaurants has been taken over by the tourist trade, but it scarcely matters. This flavorful inn was founded in 1642 and continues to serve its famous Castilian roasts: roast lamb and cured pork. Major credit cards.

La Vaca Argentina $$$-$$$$ *Cava Baja, 9; Tel. 91/366 18 60.* Open Monday-Saturday for lunch and dinner; Sunday, dinner only. Closed August. "The Argentine Cow" makes no bones about what it specializes in: grilled beef, Argentine style—caled *churrasco*. The restaurant's part of a small local chain and is full of good cheer. Take a hearty appetite. Major credit cards.

Taberna del Alabardero $$$ *Felipe V, 6; Tel. 91/547 25 77.* Open daily for lunch and dinner. A classic tavern, new by

Madrid standards (at a quarter of a century), it's a good place to visit after a night at the opera or for a rejuvenating lunch after touring the Royal Palace (both are just around the corner). It's a bustling tapas bar in the front and a select restaurant in back, serving fresh fish and exquisite meat dishes. Major credit cards.

Teatro Real $$$ *Felipe V, s/n; Tel. 91/516 06 70.* This fancy restaurant serving Spanish and continental cuisine in the newly restored opera house is rather like an upscale theme restaurant, with décor featuring costumes of famous operas and a sparkling star canopy on the ceiling. Major credit cards.

Bourbon Madrid

Champagnería Gala $-$$ *calle Moratín, 22; Tel. 91/429 25 62.* Open Monday–Friday for lunch and dinner, Saturday dinner only. A cheery place specializing in paellas and other rice dishes like risottos. Run like a coop by a group of women, it has a brightly lit and mural-covered room in front and a lively garden patio in back. An incredible bargain and favorite of Madrileños and tourists alike. No credit cards.

El Cenador del Prado $$$-$$$$ *Prado, 4; Tel. 91/429 15 61.* Open Monday–Friday for lunch and dinner, Saturday dinner only. Closed 3rd week in August. One of Madrid's most elegant restaurants, serving creative *nueva cocina española*—nouvelle Spanish cuisine. Diners can sit in either a formal salon or a garden room. Continually evolving menu and great desserts. Major credit cards.

Salamanca & Chueca Neighborhoods

El Amparo $$$$$ *Puígcerdá, 8; Tel. 91/431 64 56.* Open for dinner daily, also for lunch on weekdays. Closed the week before

Easter and month of August. A popular and elegant restaurant in the chic Salamanca barrio owned by one of the Basque country's top chefs, Martín Berasategui. If you can't make it to San Sebastián, this is the place for innovative nouvelle Basque cuisine, such as sea bass with clams and cauliflower ravioli. Major credit cards.

La Trainera $$$$ *calle Lagasca 60; Tel. 91/576 80 35.* Open Monday–Saturday for lunch and dinner. A longtime favorite with landlocked Madrileños seeking some of the freshest and best-prepared seafood in the city. Instead of roasts and suckling pig, diners delight in platters of *mariscos* (shellfish), heavenly filet of sole, and Galician-style hake. The shellfish is sold by weight. Major credit cards.

Taberna Carmencita $$ *Libertad, 16; Tel. 91/531 66 12.* Open for lunch weekdays, dinner Monday–Saturday. A classic Madrid tavern that's been in the same spot since 1840. It looks like a movie set created for a period piece, but it isn't at all touristy. Carmencita serves both traditional Castilian dishes, like cocido Madrileño, and more adverturous, Basque-influenced ones. Has a great-value weekday *menú del día*. Major credit cards.

Zalacaín $$$$ *Álvarez de Baena, 4; Tel. 91/561 48 40.* Open Monday–Friday for lunch and dinner; Saturday dinner only. Closed week before Easter and in August. The big daddy of Madrid gastronomy hasn't faltered in more than 25 years of classic dining. The menu is a mix of traditional Basque and Navarrese cooking (the chef is Basque). It'll cost you to eat here, but you're virtually guaranteed not to forget the meal. The six-course tasting menu (*menú de desgustación*) is a good deal for anyone with a hearty, yet discriminating appetite. Appropriate attire. Major credit cards.

Il Piacere Ristorante $$-$$$ *Paseo de la Castellana, 8; Tel. 91/578 34 87.* Open: Monday–Friday, lunch and dinner; Saturday, dinner only. A chic Italian place at a fashionable address, serving upscale pasta to Salamanca's in-crowd. Decent-value *menú ejecutivo*. Major credit cards.

La Galette $$ *Conde de Aranda, 11; Tel. 91/576 06 41.* Open Mon-Sat for lunch and dinner. At this cute little (mostly) vege-tarian restaurant on a quiet street near Retiro Park, the cozy din-ing rooms are always full of young people on relaxed dates. The food's inventive but affordable, given the neighborhood. Major credit cards.

Restaurante Salvador $$$ *Barbieri, 12. Tel; 91/521 45 24.* Open for lunch and dinner daily without interruption. The exte-rior couldn't be more nondescript, but it hides an Old World restaurant, its walls covered with black and white photos of bullfighters. It has several small dining rooms and does a fine job with Castilian standards like *rabo de toro* (oxen tail), fresh fish, and stuffed peppers. Major credit cards.

Bocaito $$-$$$ *Libertad, 4-6; Tel. 91/521 53 31.* Open daily for lunch and dinner. A friendly, tile-laden place in the heart of the Chueca neighborhood. You can assemble a meal from the long list of great tapas like croquettes, garlic shrimp and octo-pus, or try any of the special soups and fresh fish dishes. Major credit cards.

Sarrasin Restaurante $-$$ *Libertad, 8. Tel; 91/532 73 48.* Open daily for lunch and dinner. This attractive recent addition to the Chueca scene is always busy with locals from the design and arts communities. Excellent-value fixed-price meals for both lunch and dinner, that spice up Spanish mainstays with creative accents. Rather chic for the bargain prices. Major credit cards.

Segovia

Mesón de Cándido $$ *Plaza Azoguejo, 5; Tel. 921/42 59 11.* Open daily for lunch and dinner. This famous place, a family affair in the shadow of the glorious Roman Aqueduct, has been an inn since the early 18th century, and it was declared a national monument in 1941. It remains one of the best places to eat in Segovia. A classic meals is the *sopa castellana* "from the 15th century" and the *cochinillo* (roasted baby pig). Major credit cards.

Mesón Duque $$ *calle Cervantes, 12; Tel. 921/46 24 87.* Open daily for lunch and dinner. A classic Segovian mesón in look and feel, this cozy inn has been serving Castilian specialties like roast lamb and suckling pig since the end of the 19th century. Major credit cards.

Mesón José María $$-$$$ *Cronista Lecea, 11; Tel. 921/46 11 11.* Open daily for lunch and dinner. In front, it's a busy and friendly tapas bar, and in back, a relaxed restaurant. You can have the standard Segovian roasts or try something more adventurous, like *dorada cantábrico* — fish stuffed with garlic and mushrooms. Major credit cards.

Toledo

El Catavinos $$ *Avda. de la Reconquista, 10; Tel. 925/22 22 56.* Open daily for lunch and dinner. A simple, attractive place just outside of Toledo's old quarter, a five-minute-walk from the Bisagra gate. The focus is on diverse wines from across Spain and a wide choice of excellent-value lunch and evening fixed-price meals. Major credit cards.

Hostal del Cardenal $$-$$$ *Paseo Recaredo, 24; Tel. 925/25 07 46.* Open daily for lunch and dinner. The restaurant associated with the charming hotel of the same name has long been one of Toledo's top kitchens. With the Moorish gardens of the hotel as a backdrop, it remains one of the most pleasurable places to dine in the old city. Castilian cuisine. Major credit cards.

Restaurante Adolfo $$$ *calle de la Granada, 6; Tel. 925/22 73 21.* Open daily for lunch and dinner. Toledo's fanciest restaurant caters to locals celebrating special occasions and upscale tourists. In a 15th-century building near the cathedral—on a side street off calle Hombre de Palo—diners occupy four separate rooms. Game is a specialty of the kitchen, while the wine cellar, in an 11th-century Jewish *cueva,* or basement bodega, is the finest in the city. Major credit cards.

Restaurante Maravilla $$ *Plaza Barrio Rey, 7; Tel. 925/22 85 82.* Open daily for lunch and dinner. Part of the Hostal Maravilla, this small restaurant is decorated with colorful tiles and prepares Toledo standards like quail and partridge, as well as many different pastas, fish and shellfish. Very popular with locals. Major credit cards.

Ávila

El Molino de la Losa $$$ *Bajada de la Losa, 12; Tel. 920/21 10 01.* Open daily for lunch and dinner. The best thing about Ávila is its medieval ramparts, and you get a great view of them from this 15th-century mill, which is perched on an island in the middle of the river. The food is classic Spanish: roast suckling pig, prepared in the wood oven you see downstairs, or cuttlefish simmered in garlic and oil. Major credit cards.

Hostería de Bracamonte $$-$$$ *Bracamonte, 6; Tel. 920/25 12 80.* The restaurant connected to one of Ávila's most charming places to stay is both attractive and accomplished. The large dining room can get busy with large groups at lunchtime, when the excellent *cordero asado al horno de leña* (roast baby lamb) almost flies out of the wood oven. Good-value midday menú. Major credit cards.

INDEX